SUB FOR A HALF TITLE

I have been toying with the idea that people generally (including book collectors) tend to regard book collecting as a somewhat esoteric adventure — First Folios and such — something for Huntingtons and Folgers, and not for Smiths and Joneses. My credo is that when you own two books that are linked together by a thread of intelligence, however rudimentary, you have a book collection. Thereby every householder who owns a telephone book and a cook-book is a book collector. Thereby every village public library, however meagre, is a book collection — the thread of intelligence is service to the community. Do I mean, then, that practically everybody who owns two books is a collector? Ans.: Yes. The term "book collector" has got too tony. I think it ought to be brought back to the human level.

JOHN T. WINTERICH

BY CHARLES HONCE

BOOKS AND GHOSTS

FOR LOVING A BOOK

THE PUBLIC PAPERS OF A BIBLIOMANIAC

A VINCENT STARRETT LIBRARY

MARK TWAIN'S ASSOCIATED PRESS SPEECH

AUTHORS IN FALSEFACE

A JULIAN HAWTHORNE COLLECTION

A SHERLOCK HOLMES BIRTHDAY

WASHINGTON SQUARE

". . . the Potter's Field of the past"

From a drawing by E. H. GUNDER

BOOKS
AND
GHOSTS

A Fresh Unveiling of a Newspaperman's Literary
Preferences and Friendships

BY

CHARLES HONCE

With a True Story of Crime in Connecticut
by the Whilom Poet
JOHN T[RACY] WINTERICH

S. A. *Jacobs,* THE GOLDEN EAGLE PRESS, *Mount Vernon*

1948

For JOHN T. WINTERICH

Whose books on books Pied Pipered
me into a Delectable Land

SEE OTHER SIDE

BACK in the 1930s, when the original *Colophon* was flourishing (or at least coming out fairly regularly), it published a series of papers in which contemporary authors, American and British, described their baptisms in printer's ink. They made a distinguished company; among them were Sherwood Anderson, Robert Benchley, Stephen Vincent Benét, Theodore Dreiser, Edwin Arlington Robinson, Hugh Walpole, and Edith Wharton (to list only those, among twenty, whose pens are laid down). The stories they told were uniformly enthralling, assuming that the reader had any slightest interest in the gestation of literature, and *Colophon* readers did have.

The idea for the series was Burton Emmett's. (Burton is now with Sherwood Anderson and the others, and Burton is saying, "Now I'm just thinking out loud.") The series was known, around the shop, as "that breaking-into-print stuff," and *Breaking into Print* was the title chosen when the papers appeared in book form, in 1937, with Elmer Adler editing the units, supplying crisp biographical notes and comment, designing the book, and (inspired touch) wangling from all but four of the contributors scraps of authentic copy, to demonstrate how they worked.

Now if you have ever heard a big-game hunter tell how he was chased by a bull elephant, your subconscious forthwith flushes to the surface your own recollection of the time you were chased by a goose, and somehow, before the evening is out, you manage to work that in. Reading over the breaking-into-print papers as the manuscripts circulated around the *Colophon* shop, I naturally began to think back to my own first appearance in print. The story of that incident is utterly unimportant in itself, but it exemplifies so strongly, and quite impersonally, one universal human characteristic that I think it may be worth telling on that account, and not on mine.

I was born and spent the first ten years of my life in Middletown, Connecticut, a somnolent and elm-graced municipality whose chief claims to distinction were, and still are, Wesleyan University and an unusually wide Main Street.

There was a mild tradition of poetic composition in the family. My mother had been valedictorian of her class at Middletown High School, but instead of compounding an essay on "Integrity the Touchstone of Character," she had ingeniously elected to translate "The Legend of Sleepy Hollow" into quatrains. I have often wondered what the class poet had to say about that.

I myself was breaking into reading with Longfellow and Lowell and Whittier and Tennyson, along with *The Swiss Family Robinson,* the Grimms and Andersen, a fumigated but still engrossing *Arabian Nights,* and Jean Ingelow, whose "Seven Times One Are Seven" charmed me with its appositeness. Obviously it was written for me. So why should I not write a poem of my own?

I did. I called it "The Night." I showed it to my mother and my father and my father's sister, Aunt Bertha, who lived close by. Aunt Bertha was the sort of person who takes complete charge of everything and not only gets away with it but remains respected, admired, and adored throughout. Aunt Bertha commanded me to extend the title of my poem to "The Night and Morning." This seemed reasonable in view of the fact that five-sevenths of the composition was about morning and only two-sevenths about night.

"I want a copy of that," said Aunt Bertha. "To keep."

All unsuspecting, I accommodated her. Anybody who wanted a holograph transcript of "The Night and Morning" should have it — anybody within reason. A certain limited circulation in manuscript would be flattering and desirable and, above all, genteel. In just such furtive fashion, I learned a long time later, did Shakespeare's sonnets infiltrate into immortality.

Aunt Bertha, however, had more abrupt ideas. Middletown had two daily newspapers, the *Penny Press* and the *Tribune*. The *Penny Press* has proved the sturdier of the two — today, minus the *Penny*, it is the sole survivor. Aunt Bertha knew someone on the *Tribune*, and two or three days later, to my commingled horror and ecstasy, my poem appeared in its columns:

THE NIGHT AND MORNING

The following was composed by John Tracy Winterich, seven years old. He is the son of Mr. and Mrs. John M. Winterich:

> When the shades of night are falling,
> When the birds fly to their nest,
> And the children bright and happy
> Go to bed to have their rest.

> But the morning now is coming
> And the children will awake,
> And there is a good morning prayer
> To God, and for his sake
> To make us bright today.

> And to school the children go,
> To study work and play
> And there is no school tomorrow
> So the children may go away
> On this month of May.

I must assume that the *Tribune*'s compositor followed copy and that the rudimentary punctuation, or absence of it, was my own. I assume, too — at least I hope — that the plagiarism from Longfellow in the first line was not deliberate.

See Other Side

The only example of the original printing of this composition of whose existence I am aware (it was found among my mother's memorabilia after her death many years ago) lies before me — a not particularly yellowed scrap of paper which is undated and fails to disclose the source. (Of one-hundred home-cut newspaper clippings, ninety-nine will be undated and will fail to disclose the source.) But internal evidence ("this month of May"), coupled with the statement that the author, himself a May child, was seven years old, establishes the year as 1898.

It is something, perhaps, to have been a contemporary of Swinburne, Wilde, the early Housman (so identical with the later Housman), Crane (Stephen, not Nathalia) — of Richard Hovey, Paul Laurence Dunbar, John Bannister Tabb, Bret Harte, Lafcadio Hearn. It may be something, but that must be left for a more objective appraiser of literary influences and impetuses to determine. For, actually, "The Night and Morning" created scarcely a ripple in Middletown cultural circles (and don't think we didn't have some). True, for a day or so I was greeted with "Hello, Nightandmorning" by certain schoolfellows of low origin, and there was one brief scuffle that did not rise to the dignity of real fisticuffs. But, by and large, nothing really happened.

Why hadn't something happened, I wondered, as I contemplated the clipping the other day, half a century after its excision. After all, seven-year-old poets who actually get into print are, like two-headed calves, of infrequent occurrence. Surely a modicum of notoriety, however brief, should have resulted. Then I casually turned the clipping over and had the answer.

May I suggest an experiment. Ask a friend to time you while you hold your breath. (You can fake your part if you want to.) After he has given you the result and has put his watch back in his pocket, or his arm down, ask him what time it is. He has been staring at his watch for an appreciable period, but he has been unable to see the hour for the seconds. He cannot tell you what time it is without consulting his watch again.

Similarly, when one picks up a newspaper clipping and happens to look first at the reverse side, the lack of head or tail, or of rhyme or reason, or the general untidy look of things tells him that he *is* looking at the reverse side, and he turns quickly to the face of the clipping, the neat self-containedness of which immediately identifies it. He then reads what it is intended that he should read, and the process occludes any transient recollection of what was on the reverse.

I had always looked at "The Night and Morning" clipping without taking in the back of it. This time, I don't know why, I did take in the back. It read:

assault on Mrs. Georgiana Spencer and his trial occurred this morning. According to the evidence in court on Friday evening last Nutland's horses were found in Spencer's lot. He and his wife went to get them. Mr. and Mrs. Spencer objected. Words ensued and while Mr. Spencer was rounding up the horses so as to put them in the pound, Nutland struck his wife in the mouth, knocking out one tooth, loosening another and cutting her lip.

Nutland's version is a little different. He claims Mrs. Spencer pushed him down an embankment and hit him and kicked his wife several times. He then

See Other Side

There, I repeat, I had the answer. Palpably, the arts could not flourish in an atmosphere so highly charged with contention. Middletown, in the springtime of 1898, was in the grip of livelier affairs than the amiable and devout lyricism of a child prodigy.

I do wish, though, that the child prodigy had written a couple more stanzas.

JOHN T. WINTERICH

THIS BOOK CONTAINS

BOOKS AND GHOSTS

THE GHOSTS OF
WASHINGTON SQUARE*

March 6, 1948

WASHINGTON SQUARE is a place of dreams and ghosts.

The dreams are those of Bishop Manning and others who are trying to preserve the Square as a center of the arts.

The ghosts are those of a hundred celebrities — novelists, artists and poets — whose feet have trod the one-time Potter's Field during a century or so. They had their dreams too — heady dreams.

It looks like the appeal of New Yorkers interested in maintaining Genius Row will not prevail. People have been trying to save the rose-red brick Georgian mansions for years, but one by one the houses have fallen under the assault of tall apartment hotels and business buildings.

The north side of the Square is pretty well intact yet but the east and west sides long since have given way. The south side presents a missing tooth aspect. Somehow, it has always been the north side that has been able to sustain a graceful, if sometimes shabby, dignity.

As long ago as 1890 William Dean Howells was writing in his novel *A Hazard of New Fortunes* of the "old-fashioned American respectability which keeps the north side of the Square in vast

---

* The date at the head of each news story is that of newspaper publication. The yarns were transmitted on this continent by wire usually a week or two in advance, illustrated by photogaphs or drawings. Airmail put them elsewhere around the world in many of the more than fifty countries now served by The Associated Press. Once in a while a friend sends me a clipping from the local press of Shanghai or Calcutta or Rome. This always amazes me. However, I found out long ago that American newspapers like news stories on books, and I suppose editors in other lands have a similar reaction.

[3]

mansions of red brick and the international shabbiness which has invaded the southern border and broken it up into lodging houses, shops, beer gardens and studios."

Genius Row happens to be on the south side and it is there that another tall apartment building and a $3,000,000 law center for New York University have been planned.

So, with dreams out of the way, let's take a look at the ghosts. The ghosts, say, of Theodore Winthrop, Henry Cuyler Bunner, Robert W. Chambers, Stephen Crane, Adelina Patti, Eugene O'Neill, Edwin Arlington Robinson, William Dean Howells, Theodore Dreiser, O. Henry, Henry James, Brander Matthews, F. Hopkinson Smith, Julian Ralph and Richard Harding Davis.

All of them lived there at one time or another, or wrote of the Square and neighboring Greenwich Village.

Theodore Winthrop today is barely a footnote in the story of American letters. He was killed long ago — during the Civil War battle at Big Bethel, Virginia, in 1861. He was barely 33, but he left behind a few novels which raise the blood pressure of astute critics.

No one today knows the heartaches and the fire that went into Winthrop's books *Cecil Dreeme* and *John Brent*. George Parsons Lathrop, an earlier day American critic, described them as "among the freshest and raciest of American stories." Their author was dead before they were published.

Not even the strangely beautiful Gothic university building in which Winthrop worked and which once faced Washington Square is there any more. It was replaced many years ago by another New York University building about as aesthetically appealing as a Rutherford B. Hayes period department store. That earlier building Winthrop called Chrysalis College in his books, but it produced no butterfly.

Describing "Chrysalis," Lathrop recorded in 1886 that "the gray old University of the City on Washington Square has sheltered many a struggling poet or aspiring artist within its Norman doorways and gloomy corridors and lonesome chambers. . . . There is a small square apartment in one of the gray towers which is known, and will long be known as 'the Cecil Dreeme room.' It was there that Winthrop worked; and had he lived to mature, he would have given us much to be proud of."

Then there is the ghost of Henry James, who wrote a novel called *Washington Square*. And if you doubt the vitality of the Washington Square tradition and of the people like James who contributed to it, you have only to go over to Broadway today to learn that a play based on this tale is one of the big hits of the current theatrical season.

James described Washington Square as having "a kind of established repose which is not a frequent occurrence in other quarters of the long, shrill city; it has a richer, riper look than any of the upper ramifications of the great longitudinal thoroughfare — the look of having had something of a social history."

The building described in James' novel was the Doctor Sloper house on the north side of the Square between Fifth Avenue and Macdougal Street. Dr. Sloper had come "uptown" in 1835. Presumably the house is standing today but, if so, it has changed. This searcher, carrying a photograph taken before 1900, was unable to find its exact duplicate. Likewise, he was unable to locate the graceful building on the south side of the Square that was the scene of a Henry Cuyler Bunner romance.

Bunner (1855-1896) also died young. He once was editor of *Puck* and one of the wittiest men of his day. The Square is the locale of Bunner's novel *The Midge* (1886); and the book is drenched with the spirit of the place. Washington Square was Bunner's home in his younger Bohemian days. Throughout his brief life he seemed always to think of it with great love and sympathy.

"Bunner liked it best at night," said Arthur Bartlett Maurice, "with the great dim branches swaying and breaking in the breeze, the gas lamps flickering and blinking, when the tumults and the shoutings of the day were gone and 'only a tramp or something worse in woman's shape was hurrying across the bleak space, along the winding asphalt, walking over the Potter's Field of the past on the way to the Potter's Field to be.' "

laid out, elevated structures demolished and underground roads built to replace them."

Then, just before jumping into his tragic story, Chambers wrote: "But self-preservation is the first law, and the United States had to look on in helpless sorrow as Germany, Italy, Spain and Belgium writhed in the throes of anarchy, while Russia, watching from the Caucasus, stooped and bound them one by one."

What about the physical Washington Square? It is a sizable open space dominated by the Washington Monument, somewhat reminiscent of Paris's Arc de Triomphe. The monument was erected by the citizens of New York in 1889 to celebrate the 100th anniversary of the inauguration of George Washington as president.

From the arch, Fifth Avenue, the most aristocratic street in the world, stems northward for many miles to the Harlem River. Right after Washington Square North the avenue passes Washington Mews, once lined with the stables of the Square's aristocrats. The stables themselves now have been made over into homes for other aristocrats.

Fifth Avenue was once a street of brownstone fronts "monotonously chocolate in hue and unendingly characterless in architecture."

Back in 1863, however, this street sacred to fashion was invaded by the first tradesmen. It now is all trade from Seventh Street to the Sixties.

It has changed, and Washington Square, its source, is changing, too. It looks as though Bishop Manning has a losing fight on his hands. [And so it turned out.]

and will long be known as 'the Cecil Dreeme room.' It was there that Winthrop worked; and had he lived to mature, he would have given us much to be proud of."

Then there is the ghost of Henry James, who wrote a novel called *Washington Square*. And if you doubt the vitality of the Washington Square tradition and of the people like James who contributed to it, you have only to go over to Broadway today to learn that a play based on this tale is one of the big hits of the current theatrical season.

James described Washington Square as having "a kind of established repose which is not a frequent occurrence in other quarters of the long, shrill city; it has a richer, riper look than any of the upper ramifications of the great longitudinal thoroughfare — the look of having had something of a social history."

The building described in James' novel was the Doctor Sloper house on the north side of the Square between Fifth Avenue and Macdougal Street. Dr. Sloper had come "uptown" in 1835. Presumably the house is standing today but, if so, it has changed. This searcher, carrying a photograph taken before 1900, was unable to find its exact duplicate. Likewise, he was unable to locate the graceful building on the south side of the Square that was the scene of a Henry Cuyler Bunner romance.

Bunner (1855-1896) also died young. He once was editor of *Puck* and one of the wittiest men of his day. The Square is the locale of Bunner's novel *The Midge* (1886); and the book is drenched with the spirit of the place. Washington Square was Bunner's home in his younger Bohemian days. Throughout his brief life he seemed always to think of it with great love and sympathy.

"Bunner liked it best at night," said Arthur Bartlett Maurice, "with the great dim branches swaying and breaking in the breeze, the gas lamps flickering and blinking, when the tumults and the shoutings of the day were gone and 'only a tramp or something worse in woman's shape was hurrying across the bleak space, along the winding asphalt, walking over the Potter's Field of the past on the way to the Potter's Field to be.'"

And, recalling the pother about Genius Row, here is the concluding stanza of a poem Bunner wrote so long ago about that very spot:

> So you too are trying to find her?
> Then climb up these stairways with me.
> That twist and grow blinder and blinder,
> Till the skylight near Heaven you see.
> Is the sun my dull studio gilding?
> Oh, no, it is Kitty sits there—
> She has moved to the Studio building
> On the South side of Washington Square.

Another ghost of the Square is Robert W. Chambers. He came back to New York in 1894 at the age of 29 after studying art in Paris for seven years. But he didn't become an artist; he became a writer, and his first book of short stories, *The King in Yellow*, is saturated with Washington Square.

Scenes of two stories in the book — "The Repairer of Reputations" and "The Yellow Sign" — the latter one of the greatest horror stories ever written in America, were laid in a red brick one-time bachelor apartment building known as "The Benedick" near the southeast corner of the Square.

The building is still there but no longer is it an artists' studio and no longer does anyone care what happened to Tessie and her artist lover when the man who had been dead for months clumped up the stairs after them.

Yes, it still stands but it now is the Students' Building of New York University.

Now comes a digression, but anyone who opens "The Repairer of Reputations" today is due for a shock if he bears in mind that the story was written before 1895. It opens:

"Toward the end of the year 1920 . . . the war with Germany . . . had left no visible scars upon the republic. . . .

"Everywhere good architecture was replacing bad, and even in New York a sudden craving for decency had swept away a great portion of the existing horrors. Streets had been widened, squares

BEAUTIFUL LETTERS IN CICERO

May 15, 1948

AL CAPONE once toyed with the idea of literature — the production of his autobiography (ghost written, of course).

This yen to get his name on a book was not because of any love for beautiful letters and only partly for possible whitewashing purposes. The real incentive was money. He had the curious idea there would be millions in it.

His selected ghost writer tried to disabuse his mind of this fallacy. The project finally went on the rocks because Capone wouldn't "give." As his ghost probed the gangster's history with pointed questions, Capone replied time after time with this curious remark: "No, I couldn't say that. It wouldn't be fair to my people."

This little sidelight on the gangster era in Chicago occurred back in the Roaring Twenties. The teller of this story is Howard Vincent O'Brien. It appears in a posthumous book *All Things Considered* (Bobbs-Merrill).

O'Brien, novelist, bookman and long-time columnist for the *Chicago Daily News*, died in September 1947. He had been working on a manuscript of an autobiographical nature. The present book is made up of this material together with selections from his widely read column in the *News*.

O'Brien's introduction to Capone was real cloak-and-dagger stuff. First he received a telephone call that Capone considered him the best man to do the autobiography. Next there was a meeting with another emissary in the lobby of a South Michigan Avenue hotel: "Exactly on the stroke of one a young man appeared. He was straight out of a gangster movie, impeccably dressed and with the inevitable pearl-gray hat. He moved his head in the faintest suggestion of a nod."

[9]

reasonable honesty he was as safe as he would be in any stratum of society."

The author observes that "the gangster has many characteristics in common with the movie star and I have often wondered whether the actor imitates the gangster or vice versa."

"One of the characteristics of the gangster is his vanity and his love of publicity. One of the most successful attacks on the underworld ever made by a newspaper was when it took to referring to the silk underwear worn by some of its leaders. This really stung. Prior to that it had been the practice to refer to these characters as jailbirds and brothel keepers. The only result of this campaign was to create a new form of salutation in the underworld. When one killer met another his greeting was likely to be, 'Hi, Jailbird and brothel keeper.' But when his underwear and his eating habits were discussed he was really angry."

was indicted for evasion of his income tax and tried and sentenced to eight years in a federal penitentiary."

(The actual sentence was eleven years, of which he served seven years and six months. Capone died January 21, 1947.)

Also, O'Brien began to grow uneasy because it seemed to him "that the glances of Capone's entourage, the young men in pearl-gray hats and shoulder holsters, seemed to be looking at me with growing suspicion. Obviously I was learning a great deal more than was perhaps good for my health."

O'Brien wasn't relieved a bit when Capone said to him one day:

"You know, sometimes I lose my temper and I say, 'Gee, I wish somebody would bump that guy off,' and then one of these young punks who wants to make a name for himself goes ahead and does it. And then I have to pick up the pieces."

O'Brien got the impression that Capone was merely a cog in a machine and not a ruler. This was confirmed for him when he was called to Capone's office one day and there met three men.

"I didn't know who they were and don't know now. They sat like three shadows behind Capone and eyed me with what appeared to be cold, unfriendly eyes. Occasionally one of them would ask a question.

"I got the impression that I was being examined by the Supreme Board of Directors, and it seemed to me that behind them were probably figures still more shadowy extending on and perhaps up into the world of seeming respectability."

O'Brien also records a guess that "life in the rackets is not so dangerous as might appear.

"I got the impression that most of the gangland killings were in reality executions and, in a strange sort of way, legal. You see, in ordinary life if a man does any hurt I can sue him and gain damages in court. In the extralegal occupations, gambling, prostitution and bootlegging, the victim of an injustice has no recourse to a court. The only way he can make a man pay a bill and keep honest accounts is to threaten him with death if he fails.

"It was my impression that if a man in the rackets behaved with reasonable honesty he was as safe as he would be in any stratum of society."

The author observes that "the gangster has many characteristics in common with the movie star and I have often wondered whether the actor imitates the gangster or vice versa."

"One of the characteristics of the gangster is his vanity and his love of publicity. One of the most successful attacks on the underworld ever made by a newspaper was when it took to referring to the silk underwear worn by some of its leaders. This really stung. Prior to that it had been the practice to refer to these characters as jailbirds and brothel keepers. The only result of this campaign was to create a new form of salutation in the underworld. When one killer met another his greeting was likely to be, 'Hi, Jailbird and brothel keeper.' But when his underwear and his eating habits were discussed he was really angry."

BEAUTIFUL LETTERS IN CICERO

May 15, 1948

AL CAPONE once toyed with the idea of literature — the production of his autobiography (ghost written, of course).

This yen to get his name on a book was not because of any love for beautiful letters and only partly for possible whitewashing purposes. The real incentive was money. He had the curious idea there would be millions in it.

His selected ghost writer tried to disabuse his mind of this fallacy. The project finally went on the rocks because Capone wouldn't "give." As his ghost probed the gangster's history with pointed questions, Capone replied time after time with this curious remark: "No, I couldn't say that. It wouldn't be fair to my people."

This little sidelight on the gangster era in Chicago occurred back in the Roaring Twenties. The teller of this story is Howard Vincent O'Brien. It appears in a posthumous book *All Things Considered* (Bobbs-Merrill).

O'Brien, novelist, bookman and long-time columnist for the *Chicago Daily News*, died in September 1947. He had been working on a manuscript of an autobiographical nature. The present book is made up of this material together with selections from his widely read column in the *News*.

O'Brien's introduction to Capone was real cloak-and-dagger stuff. First he received a telephone call that Capone considered him the best man to do the autobiography. Next there was a meeting with another emissary in the lobby of a South Michigan Avenue hotel: "Exactly on the stroke of one a young man appeared. He was straight out of a gangster movie, impeccably dressed and with the inevitable pearl-gray hat. He moved his head in the faintest suggestion of a nod."

That nod carried the party to a third-floor suite. A sliding panel in the door opened slowly and a dark face looked out. The guide gave some sort of signal and the door opened.

"We were taken directly into Capone's sanctum," O'Brien says. "This resembled the office of a corporation executive. Filing cases lined the walls and there was a big desk in the bay window. Capone, as starched and pressed as a fashion plate, wearing a double-breasted brown suit, rose to greet us. He was heavily built, with an obvious tendency to fat. His manner was suave, his voice gently modulated.

"The first thing that caught my eye was the pictures on the wall behind him. One was a steel engraving of George Washington; another was a steel engraving of Abraham Lincoln. And between the two was a drawing of Capone himself wearing knickerbockers and holding a golf club."

After a get-acquainted discussion of how to play a niblick shot the talk turned to the projected autobiography. Capone "expressed his resentment at the cruel and unkind things which had been said about him."

O'Brien said he was excited by the prospect. "It seemed to me," he wrote, "that if this book were what I thought it might be made into, it would be perhaps the most significant contribution to current history that could possibly be written."

Further discussion, however, gave O'Brien a feeling of doubt about the outcome. To O'Brien's questions Capone delivered his "I couldn't say that" answer.

Additionally, "Capone had some rather exaggerated ideas as to the importance financially of the book he was to produce. He spoke lightly of millions. I pointed out that few books made millions for their authors, to which he replied blandly that there never had been a book such as this one would be."

O'Brien discussed the project with a magazine editor and they both came to the conclusion that what Capone "really wanted was not a revelation but a monument." The project thus died, helped by the fact that Capone "had more serious matters to attend to. He

BEST SELLERS AS LITERATURE

November 1, 1947

HOLD YOUR HATS, FOLKS; here's really one for the book — a literary investigator has determined that the first American best seller was the Rev. Michael Wigglesworth's "extraordinary exposition of Calvinistic theology in doggerel verse" entitled *The Day of Doom* — a product of 1662.

Or, rather it should be said that here's one from a book — *Golden Multitudes*, published this week (Macmillan), authored by Frank Luther Mott, and dealing with America's best sellers from the 285-year-old Wigglesworth opus down to Kathleen Winsor's *Forever Amber* of 1945.

Dr. Mott, Dean of the School of Journalism of the University of Missouri and Pulitzer Prize winner for American History in 1939, has produced the first detailed and rigorously tested history of the American super seller. He did it by taking plenty of time to check all available publishers' records and by using a logical and comprehensive method of selection and classification.

There have been previous compilations, starting with the 1895-1917 "Books in Demand" lists of the defunct *Bookman*, but none has been based on the wealth of data assembled by Dean Mott. As a result, he comes up with a lot of surprises, including the remarkable part detective fiction is taking in bestsellerdom; and he is able to deflate some persistent legends of astronomic sales of older books.

For instance, he estimates the world-sales of Charles M. Sheldon's celebrated religious novel *In His Steps* (1897) at 6,000,000 against some previous claims of 30 million. Also, he finds that while Horatio Alger's 135 books have sold many millions of copies, only one volume, *Ragged Dick* (1867), is found qualified for the list.

Assuming that virtually everybody has read *Forever Amber* and so knows what constitutes a modern best seller, it may be interesting to go back to Colonial times and see what people were reading then.

Mott notes that although a press was set up in Cambridge, Mass., as early as 1638, its output for the first 25 years consisted chiefly of almanacs, catechisms, sermons and hymnals, and that it did not get around "to publishing more general books that might become best sellers until the 1660s."

"When they came," he adds, "they were, of course, religious in character. Of the first twenty best sellers, twelve were designed primarily to inculcate piety and teach doctrine."

The Rev. Mr. Wigglesworth's famous poem was full of sulphur and brimstone and even touched on the theme of infant damnation — although, toward the end, there was some relenting for the "babes who had died in infancy and who were reprobates solely by the doctrine of original sin":

> ". . . therefore in bliss
> you may not hope to dwell;
> but unto you I shall allow
> the easiest room in Hell."

Dean Mott says: "It is easy to see why the Rev. Mr. Wigglesworth's opus was so popular. Its content was a theological doctrine not only universally accepted in that time and place but of the highest importance to its readers. Its presentation had an emotional drive, a vividness of imagery, and a compelling narrative movement all combined in great effectiveness. Here were verses far more sensational than the ballads about murders and hangings that were sold on the street, and Wigglesworth's influence over generations of New Englanders came largely from his shocking sensationalism."

The first edition of *The Day of Doom* was 1800 copies, nearly all snapped up within a year by what was then three per cent of the population of New England. As edition after edition came from the press, a bibliographer was able to assert the work was "more popular throughout New England for a century than any other book."

Dean Mott's roster of super best sellers (he also has a second list of "better sellers") contains 324 titles. But before he unveils them, and to "satisfy the impatience of some readers," he interpolates a list of 21 books of general reading which have enjoyed sales of more than 2,000,000 copies each in the United States and which, in his words, occupy "a kind of best seller heaven" of their own:

Alice's Adventures in Wonderland, Lewis Carroll (1866)
Ben-Hur, Lew Wallace (1880)
A Christmas Carol, Charles Dickens (1844)
Gone With the Wind, Margaret Mitchell (1936)
How to Win Friends and Influence People, Dale Carnegie (1936)
In His Steps, Charles M. Sheldon (1897)
Ishmael and sequel Self-Raised, Mrs. E. D. E. N. Southworth (1864)
Ivanhoe, Walter Scott (1820)
Last of the Mohicans, James Fenimore Cooper (1821)
Little Women, Louisa M. Alcott (1868)
Mother Goose (circa 1719)
One World, Wendell Willkie (1943)
Plays, William Shakespeare (1796 — first American publication)
The Robe, Lloyd C. Douglas (1942)
Robinson Crusoe, Daniel Defoe (1775)
See Here, Private Hargrove, Marion Hargrove (1942)
Story of the Bible, Jesse Lyman Hurlbut (1904)
Tom Sawyer, Mark Twain (1876)
Treasure Island, Robert Louis Stevenson (1884)
A Tree Grows in Brooklyn, Betty Smith (1943)
Uncle Tom's Cabin, Harriet Beecher Stowe (1852)

Dean Mott omits the Bible (actually the greatest seller of them all), prayer books, hymnals, almanacs, cook books, "doctor-books," textbooks, dictionaries and manuals. They are important, he says, but have no place in a general reading list; and he treats of them separately.

He notes that while his is a list of American best sellers, more than a third of the titles are by English authors. However, all sales were American sales and all publication dates were those of first American printings.

He sets the sales figure required to make a book a best seller at one per cent of the total population of continental United States for the decade in which the book was published. That means a sale of 1,000 before 1690 was enough to clinch a place against the almost one and a half million copies required in 1947. Today's books, however, find it comparatively easy to make the grade due to extraordinary sales through media of mass distribution such as book clubs and low-price reprints (Pocket Books alone have sold 150,000,000 copies).

Dean Mott's list settles rather emphatically the often debated question whether best sellers are literature.

"Though the lines are hard to draw," he opines, "it may be said fairly that about half the books on our best seller list have sufficient value to enable them to hold more or less assured places, at present, in the history of English and American literature.

"The long and the short of it seems to be that some best sellers are great books, while many others are good books according to ordinary literary standards. Still others — perhaps thirty per cent — fall pretty definitely outside the literary pale."

What American book fitting into Dean Mott's definition has had the greatest sale of all? For sales in this country alone he puts the finger on *Gone With the Wind;* for total world sales he hands the laurels to *Uncle Tom's Cabin.*

The former has sold more than three millions in this country and a million and a half abroad, while his world estimate for the "Iliad of the Blacks" is six and one-half millions.

A runner-up is *Ben-Hur* (1880), Lew Wallace's religious novel, which has sold about 2,600,000 copies in the United States. A mail order concern once placed an order for a million copies.

Dean Mott's book actually is a new history of American literature but dealing with many writers and trends not to be found in the usual textbook. Mrs. E. D. E. N. Southworth, for instance, is barely a footnote in literary history, yet Mott's researches crown her as "the most popular authoress in the annals of American publishing." Three of her many novels have sold two or more million copies each, and as late as 1930 a publisher listed more than 90 volumes of her work at ten cents each.

Another eye-opener for the layman is the record for murder and detective fiction. Eighteen murder mysteries find places on the top list, while many others are entered as "better sellers."

The first entry is the old favorite *The Moonstone* (1868) by Wilkie Collins, followed by the pioneer American work, *The Leavenworth Case* (1878), by Anna Katharine Green.

It was with the advent of Sherlock Holmes, however, that the detective story really got aboard the gravy-train. That was in 1890, and the going has been good ever since, with Ellery Queen down for four bell ringers and Erle Stanley Gardner for seven.

All figures pale before the record of one book — the Bible.

"It is probable," Mott says, "that there was never a year in American history in which the Bible did not excel the next-best seller. A conservative estimate of the grand total of whole Bibles distributed in the United States would place it at over two hundred million."

THE THIRTY YEARS' WAR
From a drawing by MILT MORRIS

MENCKEN *vs* THE AMERICAN
LANGUAGE

April 3, 1948

H. L. MENCKEN has pretty well conquered the American language but in the process the American language has just about conquered Mencken.

Yes, the Baltimore word wizard finally has had to consider throwing in the sponge.

Which means that with the publication today of *Supplement Two* of his monumental work on American, Mencken virtually is signing off. Like a coy presidential candidate, however, he hasn't entirely closed the door.

He says in print he probably isn't going to publish any more books on the subject, but that he will continue to collect material. In an interview he hedged on that by remarking: "If I live to be 70, I'm going to begin work on Supplement III." But that's three years off.

It's been a noble struggle, indeed! It started back in 1919 with the appearance of the first edition of *The American Language.* In the nearly thirty years since there have been six more or less distinct books as well as innumerable reprintings.

Before taking a peek into *Supplement Two,* which follows the plan of *Supplement One,* and which is keyed to the last half of the basic Fourth edition of 1936, let's have Mencken's own words on how he finally had to bow — at least for the nonce — before a seemingly unending task.

He says he had hoped to give space in *Supplement Two* to the future of American English, to present some new matter about the non-English languages, and to take up in a second appendix "certain themes not discussed at all in the Fourth edition — for example,

Mencken vs. *the American Language*

Mencken estimates that more than 95,000,000 of America's 145,000,000 speak an absolutely identical tongue. Canada likewise uses American. Even the speech of the Duke of Windsor might be considered rather closer to American than Oxford.

Three hundred years ago fewer than 5,000,000 persons spoke English. Today the figure is well over 200,000,000. And American is the lustiest buckaroo of all.

MENCKEN *vs* THE AMERICAN LANGUAGE

April 3, 1948

H. L. Mencken has pretty well conquered the American language but in the process the American language has just about conquered Mencken.

Yes, the Baltimore word wizard finally has had to consider throwing in the sponge.

Which means that with the publication today of *Supplement Two* of his monumental work on American, Mencken virtually is signing off. Like a coy presidential candidate, however, he hasn't entirely closed the door.

He says in print he probably isn't going to publish any more books on the subject, but that he will continue to collect material. In an interview he hedged on that by remarking: "If I live to be 70, I'm going to begin work on Supplement III." But that's three years off.

It's been a noble struggle, indeed! It started back in 1919 with the appearance of the first edition of *The American Language*. In the nearly thirty years since there have been six more or less distinct books as well as innumerable reprintings.

Before taking a peek into *Supplement Two*, which follows the plan of *Supplement One*, and which is keyed to the last half of the basic Fourth edition of 1936, let's have Mencken's own words on how he finally had to bow — at least for the nonce — before a seemingly unending task.

He says he had hoped to give space in *Supplement Two* to the future of American English, to present some new matter about the non-English languages, and to take up in a second appendix "certain themes not discussed at all in the Fourth edition — for example,

[21]

the language of gesture, that of children, the names of political parties, cattle brands, animal calls, and so on."

"But my notes turn out to be so enormous," he adds, "that I have been forced to close the present volume with Chapter XI, lest it grow to an impossible bulk.

"It is highly improbable that I'll ever attempt a Supplement III, but meanwhile my notes are preserved and indeed still piling up, and I may be tempted from time to time to present some of them in articles for the periodicals devoted to or showing some interest in American speech."

Mencken laments also that at his age "a man encounters frequent reminders, some of them disconcerting, that his body is no more than a highly unstable congeries of the compounds of carbon. In order to avoid fretting about this unpleasant fact I have arranged that all my books, pamphlets, journals, newspaper clippings and letters on speech shall go, at my death, to a place where they will be open to other students."

Now, let's review the rather Topsy-like way in which *The American Language* grew. The first edition, published in 1919, contained a modest 374 pages. It consisted of 1500 numbered copies, of which 25 were signed by the author.

Probably Mencken himself didn't know what he was getting into. Revised editions were required in 1921 and 1923, and each was reprinted many times.

Then came the monumental Fourth edition of 1936, which is the foundation text on which Supplements One and Two are grafted. To show more pointedly what is happening now, it needs to be recorded that the Fourth edition contained 812 pages including the index. *Supplement One,* which came out in 1945, ran to 794 pages. *Supplement Two* beats them all with 900 pages. That's a total of 2506 pages for the work in its present form. Not even *Anthony Adverse* and *Gone With the Wind* together can approach that record.

It naturally would be assumed that anyone who has plunged this deeply into the well of language would be an expert plus. And yet

Mencken vs. *the American Language*

Mencken disarmingly enough says: "I am not trained in linguistic science, and can thus claim no profundity for my book." There must be a laugh in that some place. To this writer, the complete work rates as one of the most amazing performances of the century. And, what is more, it is swell reading.

In the editions of the book prior to the Fourth, one of Mencken's themes was that English and American were progressively growing apart.

It was necessary, therefore, for the author to rewrite the Fourth edition almost entirely in order to propound his new theory that American, through the influence of the screen, stage and radio, appeared to be in the process of engulfing English English.

Boy, how the English philologians screamed at that one!

Mencken apparently hasn't changed his views. In fact, many early pages of *Supplement Two* are devoted to the spread of the American tongue, with much evidence, including quotes even from English critics, of the clear, understandable, precise, virtually uniform and beautiful language the average American uses.

Compared to it, the toniest of English "dialects," the so-called Oxford or Received Standard English of Southern England, reminds some American language students of a man trying to speak with a mouth full of marbles.

Mencken finds that a lot of this Oxford tradition with its broad "a's" and truant "r's", stems from and is fostered by the stage in England. (As a digression, it is recalled that some theatrical critics praised *Oklahoma!* when it opened in London for the clarity of its diction. One even went so far as to say it was the first time in moons an English audience was able to understand what the actors were saying.)

Whether or not American English swallows English English, it certainly is running riot around the world. And one notable thing in the country of its birth is its uniformity. Outside of some variations in the Boston area, in New York, and in parts of the South, the American tongue has a unity of pronunciation not to be matched by any other language.

Mencken vs. *the American Language*

Mencken estimates that more than 95,000,000 of America's 145,000,000 speak an absolutely identical tongue. Canada likewise uses American. Even the speech of the Duke of Windsor might be considered rather closer to American than Oxford.

Three hundred years ago fewer than 5,000,000 persons spoke English. Today the figure is well over 200,000,000. And American is the lustiest buckaroo of all.

MARK TWAIN'S "SUPPRESSED" WORKS

August 9, 1947

IF MARK TWAIN were alive today he would be the first to jump into the controversy raised by a Russian critic of American literature who recently accused "reactionary American publishers" of deliberately suppressing certain "anti-imperialist" essays by the great humorist.

For Mark Twain loved controversy, engaged in it on any appropriate occasion, and could more than take care of himself with his sledge-hammer prose.

In fact, one of the very articles referred to by Critic M. Mendelson in Moscow occasioned great controversy when it appeared at the turn of the century, and Mark, as usual, was out in the middle of the arena slugging it out with his critics in words of one syllable.

Far from being suppressed, this particular item, "To the Person Sitting in Darkness," has been rather widely printed in a variety of forms since it was originally published in *The North American Review* in 1901.

The article, which concerns the activities of missionaries in China during the Boxer Rebellion and with wars of the period, is in Mark Twain's most bitterly ironic vein. He directs machine-gun prose at all the major powers — the English in South Africa, the United States in the Philippines, the Kaiser in China, and, incidentally, Russia in Manchuria.

As an answer to his critics, who immediately pounced on him in the press, Mark came back with "To My Missionary Critics," also published in *The North American Review*, and in some ways even more biting than the original number. Regardless of the rightness or wrongness of Mark's views, the reply was evidence enough that anyone who elected to tilt with him needed a thick hide.

Mark Twain's "Suppressed" Works

"The Damned Human Race," was printed privately and anonymously in 1906 in an edition of 250 copies, copyrighted under the name of a clerk in the law offices that handled Twain's account. The first actual publication under Twain's name in this country was in 1917, seven years after his death.

The Mysterious Stranger, a satire on the human race, also was published posthumously in 1916 although Paine said it was written in 1898.

Mark Twain's writings in the social field have long received the attention of important critics. They were no late development in his career. In fact, from his earliest writing days he has commented vigorously on "Man's inhumanity to Man." Such references will be found as early as 1855 in letters he wrote for his brother Orion's Muscatine *Journal*. Mark then was 19.

A few weeks ago it was announced that Dixon Wecter, chairman of the research group at the Huntington Library at San Marino, California, had been appointed Literary Editor of the Mark Twain estate following the retirement of Mr. DeVoto from that post. DeVoto, during his editorship, compiled a considerable amount of Twain's unpublished writing, including *Mark Twain in Eruption*, originally dictated as a part of Twain's autobiography.

Wecter immediately delved into Twain's literary remains — literally hundreds of items — and several new volumes are in the offing.

The fact that there is still a great mass of unpublished Twain material does not mean suppression, however. It only means that Twain for a half century was the most prodigious worker in the whole history of American letters and piled up an overwhelming amount of writing.

As book after book appears, the total number of volumes containing first edition material by the humorist has grown to staggering proportions. The count certainly runs to three or four hundred items today.

to be merely a humorist, should now, in the light of his wider acceptance abroad, demand that he be mainly serious.

"He was serious enough, and fiercely humorous as well, in this article 'To the Person Sitting in Darkness' and in those which followed it. It seemed to him that the human race, always a doubtful quantity, was behaving even worse than usual. On New Year's Eve, 1900-01 he wrote:

" 'A Greeting From the Nineteenth To the Twentieth Century'

" 'I bring you the stately nation named Christendom, returning, bedraggled, besmirched, and dishonored, from pirate raids in Kiao-Chau, Manchuria, South Africa, and the Philippines, with her soul full of meanness, her pocket full of boodle, and her mouth full of pious hypocrisies. Give her soap and a towel, but hide the looking-glass.'

"Certain missionary activities in China, in particular, invited his attention, and in the first of the *Review* articles he unburdened himself. A masterpiece of pitiless exposition and sarcasm, its publication stirred up a cyclone."

Finally, the article was included in *The Portable Mark Twain*, published in 1946 by the Viking Press, edited by Bernard DeVoto, Twain's literary executor at the time, and containing a highlight selection from the vast totality of Mark Twain's writing.

The very fact that the editor chose this item for inclusion in a representative collection of only 786 pages is evidence of the article's literary standing among Mark Twain students and scholars.

The second article referred to by the Russian critic — "In Defense of General Funston" — originally was published in *The North American Review* for May 1902, was republished in the Tauchnitz edition of Twain's *A Double Barrelled Detective Story* in 1902, and in Twain's *Autobiography* published by Harper and Brothers in 1924.

Mark Twain himself held back some of his works or published them privately, but they have been appearing in a steady stream since the humorist's death in 1910.

For instance, *What is Man?* containing Mark's observations on

Mark Twain's "Suppressed" Works

"The Damned Human Race," was printed privately and anonymously in 1906 in an edition of 250 copies, copyrighted under the name of a clerk in the law offices that handled Twain's account. The first actual publication under Twain's name in this country was in 1917, seven years after his death.

The Mysterious Stranger, a satire on the human race, also was published posthumously in 1916 although Paine said it was written in 1898.

Mark Twain's writings in the social field have long received the attention of important critics. They were no late development in his career. In fact, from his earliest writing days he has commented vigorously on "Man's inhumanity to Man." Such references will be found as early as 1855 in letters he wrote for his brother Orion's Muscatine *Journal.* Mark then was 19.

A few weeks ago it was announced that Dixon Wecter, chairman of the research group at the Huntington Library at San Marino, California, had been appointed Literary Editor of the Mark Twain estate following the retirement of Mr. DeVoto from that post. DeVoto, during his editorship, compiled a considerable amount of Twain's unpublished writing, including *Mark Twain in Eruption,* originally dictated as a part of Twain's autobiography.

Wecter immediately delved into Twain's literary remains — literally hundreds of items — and several new volumes are in the offing.

The fact that there is still a great mass of unpublished Twain material does not mean suppression, however. It only means that Twain for a half century was the most prodigious worker in the whole history of American letters and piled up an overwhelming amount of writing.

As book after book appears, the total number of volumes containing first edition material by the humorist has grown to staggering proportions. The count certainly runs to three or four hundred items today.

MARK TWAIN'S "SUPPRESSED" WORKS

August 9, 1947

IF MARK TWAIN were alive today he would be the first to jump into the controversy raised by a Russian critic of American literature who recently accused "reactionary American publishers" of deliberately suppressing certain "anti-imperialist" essays by the great humorist.

For Mark Twain loved controversy, engaged in it on any appropriate occasion, and could more than take care of himself with his sledge-hammer prose.

In fact, one of the very articles referred to by Critic M. Mendelson in Moscow occasioned great controversy when it appeared at the turn of the century, and Mark, as usual, was out in the middle of the arena slugging it out with his critics in words of one syllable.

Far from being suppressed, this particular item, "To the Person Sitting in Darkness," has been rather widely printed in a variety of forms since it was originally published in *The North American Review* in 1901.

The article, which concerns the activities of missionaries in China during the Boxer Rebellion and with wars of the period, is in Mark Twain's most bitterly ironic vein. He directs machine-gun prose at all the major powers — the English in South Africa, the United States in the Philippines, the Kaiser in China, and, incidentally, Russia in Manchuria.

As an answer to his critics, who immediately pounced on him in the press, Mark came back with "To My Missionary Critics," also published in *The North American Review*, and in some ways even more biting than the original number. Regardless of the rightness or wrongness of Mark's views, the reply was evidence enough that anyone who elected to tilt with him needed a thick hide.

Mark Twain's "Suppressed" Works

The first reprinting of "To the Person Sitting in Darkness" was as a separate brochure, published in 1901 by the Anti-Imperialist League of New York.

Merle Johnson, Mark Twain's bibliographer, says: "If, as was claimed by the secretary of the Anti-Imperialist League, 125,000 copies of this pamphlet were distributed during the 'campaign' of 1901 as political propaganda there must have been more than one printing of the item."

Mr. Johnson continues: "Dan Beard, illustrator of *A Connecticut Yankee in King Arthur's Court,* tells of meeting Mark Twain on the street; said the author: 'By the way, I have just written something that you'll like. It is called "To the Person Sitting in Darkness." I read it to Howells [William Dean Howells], and Howells said I ought to have that published. . . . Howells also said that I must go hang myself first, and when I asked him what I should do that for, he said to save the public the trouble, because when that story appeared in print they would surely hang me.'"

Next, both magazine articles were included in a new collection of Mark Twain's work, *Europe and Elsewhere,* published posthumously in 1923 by Twain's official publishers, Harper and Brothers.

This volume was edited by Albert Bigelow Paine, Twain's biographer, who specifically referred to the missionary article in his introduction.

"Three articles in this volume," Paine wrote, "beginning with 'To the Person Sitting in Darkness,' were published at a period when Mark Twain had pretty well made up his mind on most subjects, and especially concerning the interference of one nation with another on matters of religion and government. He had recently returned from a ten years' sojourn in Europe and his opinion was eagerly sought on all public questions, especially upon those of international aspect. He was no longer regarded merely as a humorist, but as a sort of Solon presiding over a court of final conclusions.

"His old friend, W. D. Howells, expressed an amused fear that Mark Twain's countrymen, who in former years had expected him

PITY THE POOR COMPOSER!

February 21, 1948

PITY THE POOR COMPOSER of popular songs and his lyricist. They seldom are named on the radio, never on the jukeboxes and ordinarily they get only a half billing on phonograph platters.

The sheet music publisher is about the only one who exposes their full names to public gaze, but the sheet music business is not what it was in the day when the piano had no competition.

Of course, there are exceptions. Gershwin and Kern and Herbert and Rodgers and Berlin and other popular tunesmiths of like caliber usually get a plug when their compositions are played. But mostly the naming of names stops with the orchestra leader or the singer.

This, then, can be considered a sort of one man crusade to get the names of composers and lyric writers on every radio announcer's lips. Here's how it came about:

A book has just been published called *The ASCAP Biographical Dictionary of Composers, Authors, and Publishers* (Crowell). It was edited by Daniel I. McNamara, and was produced with the cooperation of the American Society of Composers, Authors, and Publishers. It contains more than 2000 biographies and tells who wrote what. You will be surprised at the identity of some of the whos in relation to some of the whats. You'll also find that while the words and music of many a piece may be familiar, the names of the authors are not — and that ain't fair.

The ASCAP book has many more virtues, however, than simply providing the text for a sermon. What probably will be most fascinating to persons who are getting along in years is the nostalgia evoked by the records of some of the old timers.

Most of them are still alive today and active. Such a one is Harry

Pity the Poor Composer!

Armstrong, composer of a number known to every American of any age. There probably is only one song that can qualify under such a sweeping statement — *Sweet Adeline*. Armstrong, born in 1879, and now living in The Bronx, is the writer of many other songs. Another easily recognizable is *I Love My Wife, but Oh You Kid!*

Back in the days when Chicago was a theatrical production center, three men wrote a series of very popular musical comedies for the old LaSalle Theater. They were Joseph E. Howard, born in 1878, Will M. Hough, 1882, and Frank R. Adams, 1883. If Howard or his one-time confreres should turn on the radio this minute it's an even chance they would hear *I Wonder Who's Kissing Her Now*.

They also collaborated on these well-remembered shows: *The Time, the Place, and the Girl, A Stubborn Cinderella, Prince of Tonight* and *Miss Nobody from Starland*. From their musical comedies came such hits as *What's the Use of Dreaming* and *Be Sweet to Me Kid*.

Hough lives in Los Angeles, Adams in Whitehall, Michigan, and Howard in New York City when he is not on the road singing, dancing and producing.

Boy, oh boy, what you can find down the musical memory lane! Here's *In the Shade of the Old Apple Tree*. Who hasn't heard of that one? It came from the pen of Egbert Anson Van Alstyne who was born in Chicago in 1882 and still lives there. All of the following songs, which are as familiar as the Woolworth Building, also were authored by Van Alstyne:

Your Eyes Have Told Me So, Won't You Come Over to My House?, I'm Afraid to Go Home in the Dark, Cheyenne, Pony Boy, Pretty Baby, and *That Old Girl of Mine.*

Cheyenne and *Pony Boy* naturally bring to mind another old timer, *Red Wing*. That was by Kerry Mills, now 79 years old and living in Hawthorne, Calif. Then there is Percy Wenrich, born in Joplin, Missouri, and now in New York, who penned *Put On Your Old Gray Bonnet*. Wenrich also wrote such barbershop-chord standbys as *Moonlight Bay, When You Wore a Tulip and I Wore a Big Red Rose,* and *Where Do We Go from Here Boys?*

Pity the Poor Composer!

You could go on like this all day among composers and songs, from Jean Schwartz and his *Chinatown,* down to the number that was put on the jukebox the day before yesterday.

Among present day musical producers who still are turning out hit tunes with the regularity of heart beats, let's pause a moment at the biography of Irving Berlin. Like Tennyson's Brook, Berlin seems to go on forever. He has written more than 1000 songs, and he qualifies for the book on all cylinders as a composer, author and publisher.

Likewise, he is a charter member of ASCAP, which was organized in 1914 by Victor Herbert and eight other "founder-members" to collect fees for public performances of copyright music.

Berlin will be 60 years old on May 11. His first song, *Marie from Sunny Italy,* came out in 1907. If in the 40 years since he has turned out more than a thousand tunes, that's at the rate of twenty-five a year or about one every two weeks. That in itself might be duplicated by another busy musician with a reasonable share of inspiration. What stands out is the tremendous number of popular successes credited to the one-time singing waiter, from *Sadie Salome, Go Home* (1907) down to the literal shower of hits in the current *Annie Get Your Gun.*

Here, although your memory probably doesn't need refreshing, are some: *What'll I Do? All Alone, Snookey Ookums, A Pretty Girl is Like a Melody, White Christmas, Alexander's Ragtime Band, They Say It's Wonderful, Easter Parade, In My Harem, When That Midnight Choo Choo Leaves for Alabam'.*

To take just one more modern composer, look over the record of Harold Arlen, who was born in Buffalo in 1905 and still is cranking up hit after hit. The reason for singling out Arlen is that (to get back to the original thesis) it is probable that few people know the full extent of his smash record. Just consider these numbers: *Stormy Weather, Devil and the Deep Blue Sea, I Love a Parade, Over the Rainbow, It's Only a Paper Moon, Blues in the Night, Accentuate the Positive, That Old Black Magic.*

The ASCAP directory reveals other surprises. Very few persons know that Rupert Hughes, novelist and playwright, also is the composer of an album of musical settings for James Whitcomb Riley's poems, in addition to a respectably long list of songs.

Then, look who's here! None other than Lionel Barrymore of the stage and screen. If he had never acted in even one movie his musical biography alone would fill a not inconsiderable space. The ASCAP dictionary notes that he was "musical from childhood, composed numerous standard pieces and made arrangements for many standard works."

His orchestral numbers include: *Russian Dances, Partita, Fugue Fantasia* and *In Memoriam*. But that isn't nearly all. There's a one-act opera, a number of piano pieces and a flock of songs, including *Johnnie Dear* and *Our Prayer*.

I suppose it is very well known that Billy Rose, nightclub impresario and latter-day columnist, has had his hand in the lyrics for a number of popular songs. The list, however, may astonish you. You'll recognize all of these: *Barney Google, That Old Gang of Mine, Rainbow 'Round My Shoulder, I Found a Million Dollar Baby in a Five and Ten Cent Store, You've Got To See Mamma Every Night, You Tell Her, I Stutter, Follow the Swallow,* and *It's Only a Paper Moon*. Not to mention the lyrics for three of Vincent Youmans' loveliest songs: *More Than You Know, Without a Song,* and *Great Day*.

And, speaking of Billy, the Roses seem to have it. There's also David Rose who wrote *Holiday for Strings;* Ed Rose who indited the words for *He Walked Right In and Turned Around and Walked Right Out Again;* Fred Rose with *Don't Bring Me Posies When It's Shoesies That I Need;* and Vincent Rose of *Avalon* and *Whispering* fame.

This story will end on a note of confusion. The ASCAP book lists two Victor Youngs, both composers and both turning out musical scores today.

The Victor Young who was born in Chicago in 1900 and who now lives in Beverly Hills, California, was responsible for such delicacies as *Stella by Starlight, Sweet Sue* and *Love Me Tonight*.

Pity the Poor Composer!

The other Victor Young was born in Bristol, Tennessee in 1889 and now is a resident of Putnam Valley, N.Y. His works for orchestra include *In the Great Smokies, Scherzetto* and *Jeep*.

I wonder if the boys speak to each other.

A MENCKEN BOOKSHELF

August 23, 1947

MOST NEWSPAPER STORIES about H. L. Mencken have to do with his pungent views on national and international questions, on the impact of his writings on American thought and on his place in American letters.

This story will sidestep all such weighty matters. It will be concerned strictly with Mencken as a collected author and will speak about his books from a physical standpoint only and have no truck whatever with what's between the covers.

That means the subject is bibliography; and the idea is pertinent today because a Mencken collector has just produced a bibliographical check-list of the Baltimorean's output over the last forty-four years.

The showing, in bulk, is impressive, as Mencken's utterances in the way of books, pamphlets, brochures, leaflets, broadsides and all other literary forms that qualify bibliographically as "books" are approaching the respectable total of 200 numbers.

The man who assembled the data is a Dartmouth college professor — Herbert Faulkner West — well known as a collector of and writer on books, and his findings occupy a chapter in his new book *The Mind on the Wing* (Coward-McCann).

West opines that it is high time somebody did the job since the last previous compilation was Carroll Frey's bibliography, published in 1924. In the 23 years since, Mencken has turned out a vast amount of work, and West has attempted to round up all the later numbers. He hasn't quite succeeded, but he is frank to say that he doubts if anybody can make a claim to absolute completeness.

Well, what does a bibliographer find? West breaks down his Mencken check-list this way:

A Mencken Bookshelf

Books, 40; books with Prefaces and Forewords, 20; contributions to other books, 35; pamphlets and broadsides, 36; pamphlets issued without date, 10. In addition, he names 22 books and pamphlets on Mencken, some of them containing Mencken writings, and 13 miscellaneous items for a grand total of 176. But that still isn't all — two new books have been published since the chapter was written and others are on the way. In this connection West says:

"Mencken has unquestionably been a vital force in contemporary letters and although his influence reached its peak perhaps in the 20s, he is still a stupendously industrious and vigorous writer."

As evidence he notes that since Mencken turned sixty he has published five books and that one of them — *Supplement I: The American Language* — which came out in 1945, sold more copies during its first three months than any other book of his.

In any consideration of a writer's productions a point of interest is his rarest book. It need not be his best; in fact quite often it is not, but it usually is the most valuable as a physical item if the author is a man of substance. Rarity in itself does not make for value.

In Mencken's case the prize is *Ventures Into Verse*. It came out in Baltimore in 1903 when the author was 23. It was printed by a couple of young fellows as a sample of typography for a newly established print shop.

It tops a Mencken collection because it happens to be his first book, because, of all things, it is poetry, and because of its extreme scarcity. Some one hundred copies were printed. Fifty went to friends of the author and publishers; the others were sent out for review or advertising purposes. Only rarely does a copy turn up today and the going price for the last twenty years has been between $150 and $200.

Here's what Mencken himself has said about this initial number in his bibliography:

"According to Vincent Starrett, who should know, my *Ventures Into Verse* is one of the rarest of modern American books. Every now and then I hear of a sale at a fantastic price; the last one, as I recall it, was beyond $150. Such news naturally caresses an author's gills; nevertheless, I find myself somewhat disquieted, for the book, in the main, is dreadful stuff and any buyer who happens to be a man of taste must needs conclude that he has been rooked, and lay some of the blame for the swindle upon me. In my defense, I can only say that I was young when the thing was published and even younger when most of it was written and that the wisdom which now radiates from me was late in developing."

Other Mencken books which West says are rather difficult to find are: *George Bernard Shaw* (1905); *Pistols for Two* (1917); *The Philosophy of Friedrich Nietzsche* (1908); *Damn! A Book of Calumny* (1918); *In Defense of Women* (1918); *A Little Book in C. Major* (1916); *A Book of Prefaces* (1917); *The Artist* (1912); and *A Book of Burlesques* (1916).

First editions of *The American Language* also are scarce since only 1500 copies were printed in 1919.

The bibliography of any active writer always includes a hatful of ephemerae in which only the collector and possibly the author are very much interested. Mencken's *opera* are rich in such items. Here are a few of his odd numbers, taken at random from the 176 entries:

"96. Baltimore, issued by the Baltimore Canned Goods Exchange in 1914 as an invitation to that city. Contains 'Good Old Baltimore,' by Mencken."

"111. The Rewards of Virtue, by H. L. Mencken. Reprinted by Baltimore Evening Sun, 1925."

"114. Sterling, by H. L. Mencken. A large single sheet printed by John Henry Nash for his friends. An essay on George Sterling (1926)."

"138. What Mencken Thinks of El Paso and Juarez. Published by Central Cafe, Juarez, Mexico (no date)."

There are dozens of such items; but only a really rabid Mencken collector will go out gunning for them.

It is a question who has the most extensive Mencken collection. Possibly it is Paul Patterson, publisher of the Baltimore *Sun*, who

aged to amass, at different times, three book collections, one of which still is with him.

Mencken's feeling about book collecting came out when a friend, who was bringing out a book on books, asked him for a short Introduction. He replied that he would be delighted to provide one, but added: "I have never been a book collector; perhaps my reasons for that might be interesting, though they are trivial."

Mencken's Introduction, which arrived in due course, was accompanied by a letter which reveals Mencken's views on the non-sanctity of his prose: "The enclosed is all I seem to be able to squeeze out of the subject of book collecting. The truth is that I know relatively little about it. If you want this piece it is yours. If not, please don't hesitate to say so. You are, of course, free to cut it down to fit your space. I hold the world's record in one respect at least: In 46 years of newspaper work I have never complained about anything done by a copy-reader."

But to get back to collecting. Many potential collectors are steered away by the feeling that book gathering is an extremely expensive business. Generally, this is not so. A few obscure items of any active author usually are difficult to obtain and sometimes quite expensive. The general run, however, will yield to a little digging. As to Mencken, West says:

"The diligent collector can build up an excellent Mencken collection without mortgaging his future."

recall it, was beyond $150. Such news naturally caresses an author's gills; nevertheless, I find myself somewhat disquieted, for the book, in the main, is dreadful stuff and any buyer who happens to be a man of taste must needs conclude that he has been rooked, and lay some of the blame for the swindle upon me. In my defense, I can only say that I was young when the thing was published and even younger when most of it was written and that the wisdom which now radiates from me was late in developing."

Other Mencken books which West says are rather difficult to find are: *George Bernard Shaw* (1905); *Pistols for Two* (1917); *The Philosophy of Friedrich Nietzsche* (1908); *Damn! A Book of Calumny* (1918); *In Defense of Women* (1918); *A Little Book in C. Major* (1916); *A Book of Prefaces* (1917); *The Artist* (1912); and *A Book of Burlesques* (1916).

First editions of *The American Language* also are scarce since only 1500 copies were printed in 1919.

The bibliography of any active writer always includes a hatful of ephemerae in which only the collector and possibly the author are very much interested. Mencken's *opera* are rich in such items. Here are a few of his odd numbers, taken at random from the 176 entries:

"96. Baltimore, issued by the Baltimore Canned Goods Exchange in 1914 as an invitation to that city. Contains 'Good Old Baltimore,' by Mencken."

"111. The Rewards of Virtue, by H. L. Mencken. Reprinted by Baltimore Evening Sun, 1925."

"114. Sterling, by H. L. Mencken. A large single sheet printed by John Henry Nash for his friends. An essay on George Sterling (1926)."

"138. What Mencken Thinks of El Paso and Juarez. Published by Central Cafe, Juarez, Mexico (no date)."

There are dozens of such items; but only a really rabid Mencken collector will go out gunning for them.

It is a question who has the most extensive Mencken collection. Possibly it is Paul Patterson, publisher of the Baltimore *Sun*, who has been intimately associated with Mencken on the *Sunpapers* for many years.

However, other collectors are convinced that their gatherings are tops. One is the Dartmouth College Library (West's check-list was mainly compiled from Dartmouth's Richard H. Mandel Collection).

"We have, I believe," said Harold G. Rugg, assistant librarian, "the very largest and finest Mencken collection of any library in the country. This collection was given to us by one of our alumni a few years since and Mr. Mencken has been adding to it very regularly, sending us rare and obscure articles together with manuscripts."

Incidentally, Mr. Rugg mentioned that the books are "housed in the Treasure Room of the library."

Bradford F. Swan, of the Providence *Journal* and *Evening Bulletin,* is equally proud of his collection.

"My Mencken is, I honestly believe, the best in existence, being especially strong in ephemeral material," he says. "HLM himself seems to agree with me on this; but he is the one who deserves the credit, for he has been most generous in helping to build it. It is not now, and never will be, for sale; I have worked 18 years putting it together with the idea of depositing it eventually at Yale, my Alma Mater." [Some of Swan's material already has been transferred to the Yale Library.]

(Parenthetically, Princeton is not asleep. Through Julian Boyd it is assembling a collection of Mencken letters.)

Thus it will be seen that Mr. Mencken has extended a helping hand to several collectors of his books.

Whether he has a full set of his own first editions is debatable inasmuch as he has said that "I have never thought of myself as a book collector."

"If there are such things as inadvertent book collectors, then I seem to belong to the clan," he said recently. "Never in this life have I bought a book for its age or rarity or elegance alone. . . ."

However, as an aside, it might be mentioned that Mencken man-

GEORGE GERSHWIN'S MONUMENT

January 31, 1947

ARE YOU STILL playing, singing or listening to the music of George Gershwin?

The chances are that the answer is Yes since Gershwin's music is more popular today — eleven years after the composer's death — than ever before.

Can it be possible that the onetime Tin Pan Alley tunesmith, who died tragically young at 38, will turn out to be America's most enduring composer?

The long-haired boys may be expected to hem and haw or to record a prompt No! But the record of Gershwin's continuing and increasing popularity is something you just don't casually shrug off.

But regardless of where Euterpe finally bestows her toppest accolade, the fact remains that probably the most widely known and popular modern composition by an American is a Gershwin work.

That number is *Rhapsody in Blue.*

The subject is particularly apropos at this time because the *Rhapsody* will have a birthday on February 12 — its twenty-fourth. Curiously, that is pretty close to the age of the composer when he hurriedly turned it out on commission from Paul Whiteman in 1924.

The piece hit the critics like a ton of bricks. It hit the general public even harder. Today it is probably the biggest platter seller among concert pieces by a native American; it is a constant favorite on the air; it is widely performed by orchestras, and it is popular with almost every pianist who can run a glissando without breaking a finger.

In evidence is the fact that the *Rhapsody* placed both second and third on *Billboard*'s recent compilation of 1947's "Top Selling to a Gershwin book. In it Whiteman had this further comment:

"Somewhere in the middle of the score (*Rhapsody in Blue*) I began crying. When I came to myself I was eleven pages along, and until this day I cannot tell you how I conducted that far. Afterwards George told me he experienced the same sensation. He cried, too."

There have been several versions of the composition and scoring of the *Rhapsody*. The most romantic is that George forgot all about the business until he happened to read in a newspaper column that he was supposed to be busily engaged on a symphonic work. Then, with only ten days to go, he plunged in.

Actually, Gershwin spent more time than that, but the fact remains that it was a hurry-up struggle, that Ferde Grofé, who was responsible for the orchestration, literally pulled the manuscript page by page from the composer's hand, and that on the night of February 12 there still were a few blank spots in the piano sections. But Gershwin was to be at the piano and could take care of that.

At that the time of Gershwin's death in 1937 critics debated whether his eventual fame would stem from the musical comedy stage or the concert hall. The question is pretty well decided now. The evidence is on the side of the concert hall.

The record shows that such orchestral works as the *Rhapsody*, the lovely *Concerto in F, An American in Paris,* and the *Porgy and Bess* music are head and heels in front of the greater part of the work Gershwin did in musical comedy.

It also is somewhat odd that of the hundreds of songs Gershwin wrote for Broadway, probably not more than a score are heard to any great extent today. In that score are some honeys which may hang on for a long time, but they're going to have hard sledding to keep within bowing distance of the first *Rhapsody*.

Apparently the true Gershwin addict likes a mixture of the composer's heavier and lighter pieces. Seventeen thousand such Gershwinites annually pack Lewisohn Stadium in New York on all-Gershwin nights.

The high point is always *Rhapsody in Blue.*

Whiteman faced the loss of the money with far more equanimity than the thought of facing his very distinguished audience. In short, he was just about scared to death.

"Fifteen minutes before the concert was to begin," Whiteman has recorded, "I yielded to a nervous longing to see for myself what was happening out front, and putting an overcoat over my concert clothes, I slipped around to the entrance of Aeolian Hall.

"There I gazed upon a picture that should have imparted new vigor to my wilting confidence. It was snowing, but men and women were fighting to get into the door, pulling and mauling each other as they do sometimes at a baseball game, or a prize fight, or in the subway. Such was my state of mind by this time, that I wondered if I had come to the right entrance. And then I saw Victor Herbert going in. It was the right entrance, sure enough, and the next day, the ticket office people said they could have sold out the house ten times over.

"I went back stage again, more scared than ever. Black fear simply possessed me. I paced the floor, gnawed my thumbs and vowed I'd give $5000 if we could stop right then and there. Now that the audience had come, perhaps I had really nothing to offer them at all. I even made excuses to keep the curtain from rising on schedule. But finally there was no longer any way of postponing the evil moment. The curtain went up and before I could dash forth, as I was tempted to do, and announce that there wouldn't be any concert, we were in the midst of it.

"It was a strange audience out in front. Vaudevillians, concert managers come to have a look at the novelty, Tin Pan Alleyites, composers, symphony and opera stars, flappers, cake-eaters, all mixed up higgledy-piggledy."

Whiteman came by his agitation honestly enough. In addition to Victor Herbert, musical notables present included Walter Damrosch, Heifetz, Godowsky, Kreisler, McCormack, Rachmaninoff, Sousa and Stokowski, as well as all the first-string music critics.

Soon after Gershwin's death, many persons whose paths had crossed that of the late composer contributed reminiscences to a Gershwin book. In it Whiteman had this further comment:

"Somewhere in the middle of the score (*Rhapsody in Blue*) I began crying. When I came to myself I was eleven pages along, and until this day I cannot tell you how I conducted that far. Afterwards George told me he experienced the same sensation. He cried, too."

There have been several versions of the composition and scoring of the *Rhapsody*. The most romantic is that George forgot all about the business until he happened to read in a newspaper column that he was supposed to be busily engaged on a symphonic work. Then, with only ten days to go, he plunged in.

Actually, Gershwin spent more time than that, but the fact remains that it was a hurry-up struggle, that Ferde Grofé, who was responsible for the orchestration, literally pulled the manuscript page by page from the composer's hand, and that on the night of February 12 there still were a few blank spots in the piano sections. But Gershwin was to be at the piano and could take care of that.

At that the time of Gershwin's death in 1937 critics debated whether his eventual fame would stem from the musical comedy stage or the concert hall. The question is pretty well decided now. The evidence is on the side of the concert hall.

The record shows that such orchestral works as the *Rhapsody,* the lovely *Concerto in F, An American in Paris,* and the *Porgy and Bess* music are head and heels in front of the greater part of the work Gershwin did in musical comedy.

It also is somewhat odd that of the hundreds of songs Gershwin wrote for Broadway, probably not more than a score are heard to any great extent today. In that score are some honeys which may hang on for a long time, but they're going to have hard sledding to keep within bowing distance of the first *Rhapsody.*

Apparently the true Gershwin addict likes a mixture of the composer's heavier and lighter pieces. Seventeen thousand such Gershwinites annually pack Lewisohn Stadium in New York on all-Gershwin nights.

The high point is always *Rhapsody in Blue.*

GEORGE GERSHWIN'S MONUMENT

January 31, 1947

ARE YOU STILL playing, singing or listening to the music of George Gershwin?

The chances are that the answer is Yes since Gershwin's music is more popular today — eleven years after the composer's death — than ever before.

Can it be possible that the onetime Tin Pan Alley tunesmith, who died tragically young at 38, will turn out to be America's most enduring composer?

The long-haired boys may be expected to hem and haw or to record a prompt No! But the record of Gershwin's continuing and increasing popularity is something you just don't casually shrug off.

But regardless of where Euterpe finally bestows her toppest accolade, the fact remains that probably the most widely known and popular modern composition by an American is a Gershwin work.

That number is *Rhapsody in Blue.*

The subject is particularly apropos at this time because the *Rhapsody* will have a birthday on February 12 — its twenty-fourth. Curiously, that is pretty close to the age of the composer when he hurriedly turned it out on commission from Paul Whiteman in 1924.

The piece hit the critics like a ton of bricks. It hit the general public even harder. Today it is probably the biggest platter seller among concert pieces by a native American; it is a constant favorite on the air; it is widely performed by orchestras, and it is popular with almost every pianist who can run a glissando without breaking a finger.

In evidence is the fact that the *Rhapsody* placed both second and third on *Billboard's* recent compilation of 1947's "Top Selling

Classical Record Albums Over Retail Counters," based on weekly reports from 1000 retailers.

The Number One item was Rachmaninoff's *Concerto No. 2 in C Minor,* but as the total points scored for second and third places top the Rachmaninoff number, it is to be presumed that Gershwin actually led the field. The second place recording was that of the Philadelphia Orchestra, directed by Eugene Ormandy and with Oscar Levant at the piano. The third place recording was by the man who started it all — Paul Whiteman.

Gershwin died in Hollywood of a brain tumor on July 11, 1937. He was born in Brooklyn on September 26, 1898, and so would have been only 49 today.

It is idle to speculate what heights he might have scaled had he been spared for eleven more years of composition. Probably it is enough to say that in a comparatively brief career he was able to win a unique place in American music. However, it is worth noting that while his *Second Rhapsody* (1931) is a comparatively minor effort, and his *Cuban Overture* (1934) is no great shakes among his larger works, he actually was at the peak of his powers in his last major production. This was the folk opera *Porgy and Bess* (1935).

It was only eleven years before *Porgy* that he sounded his first great musical challenge. And there is no doubt that that earlier date — February 12, 1924 — was a momentous occasion in the history of American music. For it was on this Lincoln's Birthday afternoon that Paul Whiteman elected to present his jazz concert in Aeolian (not Carnegie) Hall.

The program included a new and graceful *Suite of Serenades* by Victor Herbert and examples of jazz in a variety of forms. But what made the afternoon memorable was the *Rhapsody.*

Historians of the famous occasion record that Whiteman spared no expense to put a top hat on jazz. From his augmented orchestra down to the program book the concert cost $11,000. Whiteman's loss, in spite of the fact that the auditorium could have been packed many times over, amounted to $7000.

"Bookworms!"

From a drawing by R. Taylor *in* The New Yorker

REDRAWN BY PERMISSION
(HALFTONE TO LINE)

Copyright, 1946, The F-R Publishing Corporation

GEORGE ADE AND THE
LIFE OF RILEY

February 29, 1948

GEORGE ADE, if you could only see the book that was published about you today you surely would rub your eyes and say it must be a Fable!

A story as fantastic, in fact, as any of the scores of *Fables in Slang* you turned out in your writing days.

The book is a bibliography of your writings and it takes some 300 pages to list them definitively.

That means that you must have been a prodigious worker back when you were burning up a typewriter. Why? Because you were able to do what so many people dream of but seldom achieve: retire at a reasonably early age and just sit back and enjoy yourself. . . .

The title is *A Bibliography of George Ade* (1866-1944), compiled by Mrs. Dorothy Ritter Russo, and published by the Indiana Historical Society at Indianapolis.

With the exception of a patent medicine ad or two which Mrs. Russo was unable to trace, the volume contains a record of virtually everything Ade wrote from such an intriguing title as *Handsome Cyril, or The Messenger Boy with the Warm Feet* down to the last thing that came from his pen before his death on May 16, 1944.

George Ade was able to lay by quite a bunch of lettuce through his books and particularly through his plays and musical comedies such as *The Sultan of Sulu* (1902), *The Sho-Gun* (1904), and *The College Widow* (1905). That enabled him to develop his magnificent Hazelden Farm near Brook, Indiana, and proceed to live the life of Riley. For probably 25 years before his death he did comparatively little writing, but nevertheless his bibliography is one of real magnitude.

Mrs. Russo records 55 books, plays, and pamphlets of major importance; 44 "ephemeral publications"; 95 contributions to books and pamphlets; and seven reprint editions. That's a total of 201 items.

In addition, 31 books, pamphlets and leaflets have been written about Ade. And nine pages of small type are required to record the names of periodicals containing articles about the humorist. But the biggest compilation of all is a section of 96 pages listing the magazines and newspapers with first appearances of Ade's writing. Incidentally, a large number of his stories, particularly those which appeared in newspapers, never have been collected in book form. That means there may be happy hunting ahead for some editor.

This bibliographical operation by the Indiana Historical Society is pretty close to unique. Usually it is only top flight authors such as Poe or Hawthorne who are the subjects of full dress bibliographies. This is because a bibliography largely is a labor of love, is costly to compile, costly to publish and has a limited chance of circulation.

Out in Indiana, however, the Lilly Endowment, Inc., has been set up by a wealthy industrial family which also likes books; and one of the Endowment's projects covers the production of bibliographies of Indiana authors. A previous book covered the writings of the Hoosier poet James Whitcomb Riley. It came out in 1944.

Ade was born in 1866 within 15 miles of the place where he died. His first writings were for Lafayette, Indiana, newspapers. These have not been clearly identified. He went to Chicago in 1890, and Mrs. Russo notes that "the ten years of Ade's connection with Chicago newspapers . . . saw a prolific output from his mind and pen." Out of the columns of the old Chicago *Record* came his first books and he went back to the same source for later ones.

An Ade column, which ran almost daily in the *Record* for a seven-year period beginning in 1893, "Stories of the Streets and of the Town," provided material for many of Ade's volumes including a series of eight pamphlets published by the newspaper between 1894 and 1900.

None of these carried Ade's name and this is the first time they have ever been mentioned in any bibliographical check-list of the humorist's work. That, incidentally, is what bibliography is for— to search out every piece of writing in every form by a given author and to describe it so accurately that there can be no dispute as to its first edition form.

Mrs. Russo and those who assisted her in her delving have brought to light a number of other Ade oddities. One is *Circus Day,* written for the "Little Folks Library" in 1896. The leaf measures two and three-eighths by two and three-sixteenths inches. The first issue of *Circus Day* is described as almost legendary. Another miniature book of the same size is *Stories from History* written under the pseudonym of John Hazelden.

Both of these curious little volumes were illustrated by John T. McCutcheon, the famous cartoonist, who was associated with Ade in several other productions.

Ade probably is best remembered by his *Fables in Slang* (1900) and by a succession of similar collections, such as *More Fables* (1900), *Forty Modern Fables* (1901), and *Hand-made Fables* (1920).

However, a lot of other Ade numbers readily will be recalled, including *Artie* (1896), *Pink Marsh* (1897), *Doc' Horne* (1899), *True Bills* (1904), and *The Slim Princess* (1907).

The latter was Ade's only long fiction. It first appeared as a short story in a magazine. Then it was lengthened into a novelette. Next it was made into a play. Later it turned up as a musical comedy with Elsie Janis. Finally, the movies filmed it twice.

Ade turned out a lot of plays and wrote the librettos and lyrics for many musical comedies. Probably his most successful play was *The College Widow,* first produced in 1905 but which did not appear in book form until 1924. This likewise was made into a musical comedy and two movies.

Ade said of this play: "During the first three weeks after I settled in my new home (Hazelden) and reveled for the first time in wide expanses of elbow-room and a real sense of proprietorship, I made up for lost time and turned out a play called *The College Widow*. It was approved by the public and never had to be revised as it did over two million dollars at the box-office before it went to the stock companies."

Among Ade's original musical comedies, the music for *The Sho-Gun* and *The Fair Co-ed* (1908) came from Gustav Luders, a leading writer of light operas of the period and the composer of the well-remembered *The Burgomaster*.

Dyed-in-the-wool collectors always like to lay their hands on such rare and obscure items as *Handsome Cyril*. That was one of three booklets in the "Strenuous Lad's Library," each running to 28 pages and printed in Phoenix, Arizona, in small editions. The take-off on Horatio Alger is obvious. The others bear these equally compelling titles: *Clarence Allen, the Hypnotic Boy Journalist, or the Mysterious Disappearance of the United States Government Bonds,* and *Rollo Johnson, the Boy Inventor, or the Demon Bicycle and Its Daring Rider.*

These three, together with other items of a similar nature from the old Chicago *Record,* were reprinted years later in Ade's book *Bang! Bang!* (1928).

It is also interesting that the last full-length book that appeared before Ade's death was called *Stories of the Streets and of the Town.* This was a special edition published by the Caxton Club of Chicago in 1941, but reproducing newspaper stories written by Ade between 1894 and 1900.

Just because Ade didn't do a great deal of writing in his later years does not mean that he was not busy at one thing or another.

"Ever since I settled down in the country," Ade wrote in 1942, "I have been involved in activities which did not call my name to the attention of the general public but which have been an interesting part of my career. For quite a number of years I have paid more attention to these activities than I have to writing. . . .

"My enthusiasms include golf, travel, horse racing and the spoken drama. My antipathies are social show-offs, bigots on religion, fanatics on total abstinence, and all persons who take themselves seriously. I won't let myself become a moss-back or a has-been. . . .

"I have a card-index memory for the words and music of old songs. I love to put on big parties or celebrations and see a throng of people have a good time. I do not choose to make speeches or listen to speeches."

That sounds like a pretty good program. With it, and with his books, George Ade provided a good time for lots of people. One of his admirers was Mark Twain, who said this of Ade's book *Pink Marsh:*

"Pink-Oh the shiftless, worthless, lovable black darling! He deserves to live forever. Mark."

NOSTALGIA UNLIMITED

October 18, 1947

Is IT NOSTALGIA — that groping for the illusive rainbow of the past — that is back of all these "revivals"? Or did the boys of an older generation have something that can't quite be duplicated today?

There is no profit in trying to answer such questions. But let's see what the record shows.

George Bernard Shaw, still very much alive and busy with his pen at 91, conjured *Man and Superman* out of his playbag almost a lifetime ago (1903).

It's news again today because an astute producer had the happy inspiration to revive it. The revival, last week, turned out to be so good that Brooks Atkinson recorded in the New York *Times* that "by the simple device of dipping back a half century in dramatic literature, Maurice Evans has given the season its first crackle of brilliance." Other critics were equally enthusiastic.

But it is not only in the theater that the dear dead past is being evoked. Even the jukeboxes have a tale to tell, or, more to the point, a song to sing — as witness the renewed and vigorous youth of *Peg o' My Heart,* and other melodies of earlier day tunesmiths.

Then, again, vaudeville is showing new stirrings of life, while the amateur radio show, popularized by the late Major Bowes, is on the comeback trail.

The trend is not so pronounced in the bailiwick of books — at least no outstanding novel of a past generation is currently battling for top place on the best-seller list. However, an interesting fact is that in literature the great and near great books of mankind's discernible past never die and therefore need no specific revival. Edition after edition of works that have stood up under the weather-the aeons. No one has to "revive" Rembrandt, Raphael or Rubens. However, there often are sub-currents of renewed interest in painters of a generation or two back, and this is in evidence today in the attention paid to Thomas Eakins (1844-1916), Winslow Homer (1836-1910) and others of their period. In the case of these artists the interest undoubtedly has a tinge of nostalgia since they flourished in a period known and loved by many people still alive although presently not too agile.

There are two fields in which it might be said there never is a revival — because of the persistence of a pattern.

One is the opera and the other is the classic ballet. The routine of the ballet has changed but little from the day an individual first found it was possible to dance on his (or her) toes or leap into the air and land without falling on his nose.

And, if you subscribe to an opera season, you invariably know just what to expect.

NOSTALGIA UNLIMITED

October 18, 1947

Is it NOSTALGIA — that groping for the illusive rainbow of the past — that is back of all these "revivals"? Or did the boys of an older generation have something that can't quite be duplicated today?

There is no profit in trying to answer such questions. But let's see what the record shows.

George Bernard Shaw, still very much alive and busy with his pen at 91, conjured *Man and Superman* out of his playbag almost a lifetime ago (1903).

It's news again today because an astute producer had the happy inspiration to revive it. The revival, last week, turned out to be so good that Brooks Atkinson recorded in the New York *Times* that "by the simple device of dipping back a half century in dramatic literature, Maurice Evans has given the season its first crackle of brilliance." Other critics were equally enthusiastic.

But it is not only in the theater that the dear dead past is being evoked. Even the jukeboxes have a tale to tell, or, more to the point, a song to sing — as witness the renewed and vigorous youth of *Peg o' My Heart,* and other melodies of earlier day tunesmiths.

Then, again, vaudeville is showing new stirrings of life, while the amateur radio show, popularized by the late Major Bowes, is on the comeback trail.

The trend is not so pronounced in the bailiwick of books — at least no outstanding novel of a past generation is currently battling for top place on the best-seller list. However, an interesting fact is that in literature the great and near great books of mankind's discernible past never die and therefore need no specific revival. Edition after edition of works that have stood up under the weathering of time come out year after year. Mark Twain is just as popular now as he was in the day when his books were plumping fresh from the presses. Dickens, Balzac, Shakespeare, Poe and others on a list as long as your arm continue as steady sellers.

Nevertheless, there is at least a hint of the "revival" idea in the book trade. One publisher has just brought out a volume by that one hundred per cent mid-Victorian — Anthony Trollope (1815-1882) — and another has produced a book housing three "Victorian" novels. There will be plenty of nostalgia there for some.

Henry James (1843-1916), the tortured stylist of American realism, likewise has suddenly come to the front. Several of his novels currently have been reprinted, a couple of books have been written about him, and the atmosphere of his period and of his writing was duplicated in a newly produced play, *The Heiress,* based on his novel, *Washington Square* (1881).

Another interesting straw in the wind is the fact that a new edition of *Three Soldiers* (1921), authored by John Dos Passos shortly after World War I, has just hit the book stores at a time when the first flush of interest in World War II books is beginning to wear off.

The Shaw revival is one of the most provocative items in the picture. The Irish dramatist, who never has been crowned for modesty, always has maintained that he is just about the greatest playwright in the world and to be classed only with a fellow named Shakespeare. The fact that his close to a half-century-old drama could come back to Broadway and capture audiences and close-to-rave notices in the newspapers is evidence that the old boy undoubtedly has something there, particularly as the play was staged at the tail end of a dismal succession of turkeys by modern-day dramatists.

The current Shaw success follows a similar pattern of other recent Shaw revivals, including *Candida* (originally produced in 1898) and *Pygmalion* (1912). In the same boat were last season's well-applauded revivals of Oscar Wilde's *The Importance of Being Earnest* (1899) and *Lady Windermere's Fan* (1893).

Nostalgia Unlimited

The stage also has produced evidences of nostalgic appeal on the American side of the fence in the recent long-time runs of Victor Herbert's *The Red Mill* (1906) and *Sweethearts,* of 1913 vintage.

The sharpest impact of the revival undoubtedly is in the field of popular music and by way of two fairly modern inventions, the radio and the jukebox.

In addition to *Peg o' My Heart* (1913), three other songs — *I Wonder Who's Kissing Her Now* (1909), *When You Were Sweet Sixteen* (1898), and *Heartaches* (1931) have been assaulting America's ears for weeks.

"No one," says Douglas Gilbert * in the New York *World-Telegram,* "has advanced a reason for the sudden popularity of the old-time tunes. That they are pleasing melodies, new to the current crop of listeners may be one explanation. That their lyrics express a contrasting and comfortable sentiment to the tailspin world we live in may be another."

Certainly these songs have quite simple melodies and lyrics as contrasted with the more complex rhymes and rhythms of today. That means that both words and music are easy to remember and thus can be hummed, sung, whistled or crooned by people who find that some present day songs, while sounding comparatively simple in the hands of an orchestra, are pretty difficult to negotiate when tried out in the bathroom.

Gilbert also finds that these revivals have had an unusual economic effect:

"A number of the younger writers," he relates, "virtually have been forced out. Some of these are cynical, some blasé, most are reasonably intelligent, skeptical of June-moon rhyming, and disdain simple tunes of only two or three harmonic changes. The youngsters, one publisher complains, still are writing for swing bands when they should be trying for singable tunes with guileless lyrics, the vogue now."

Art, like literature, finds its masterpieces appreciated through

* Gilbert died untimely in 1948.

[55]

the aeons. No one has to "revive" Rembrandt, Raphael or Rubens. However, there often are sub-currents of renewed interest in painters of a generation or two back, and this is in evidence today in the attention paid to Thomas Eakins (1844-1916), Winslow Homer (1836-1910) and others of their period. In the case of these artists the interest undoubtedly has a tinge of nostalgia since they flourished in a period known and loved by many people still alive although presently not too agile.

There are two fields in which it might be said there never is a revival — because of the persistence of a pattern.

One is the opera and the other is the classic ballet. The routine of the ballet has changed but little from the day an individual first found it was possible to dance on his (or her) toes or leap into the air and land without falling on his nose.

And, if you subscribe to an opera season, you invariably know just what to expect.

PAGING CHARLES DUDLEY WARNER

You are now about to get on a literary merry-go-round.
You'll go round and round and round and end up just
about where you started. However, the chronological
method is about the only way this serial story can be told
without messing it up entirely.

August 30, 1947

IT'S DOLLARS to doughnuts you don't know who said:

"Everybody talks about the weather, but nobody does anything
about it."

Mark Twain you say?

No. A thousand times no!

Mark never even came near such a declaration although for years
he has been widely credited with uttering it.

To get to the point, the real author was Charles Dudley Warner,
a humorist of parts during the latter part of the last century.

The only reason the subject comes up at this time is because
the writer has heard the remark hung on Mark Twain three times
in recent days — on the radio, in a book, and in a news story.

That seems to give the matter sufficient currency to warrant
an attempt to try to set the business right and possibly to clear
the record for the future. It is not likely, however, that any such
thing will happen.

Like H. L. Mencken's burlesque history of the bathroom, which
got picked up generally and persists to this day in spite of the fact
that Mencken has exploded the whole story, it is to be presumed

that Mark Twain, through all days to come, still will be called the author of one of the most widely known quotations of modern days.

It is difficult to arrive at any satisfactory explanation why Warner was deprived of credit for his coinage. The nearest approach to a solution is in the fact that both Warner and Twain were humorists, once lived near each other in Hartford, Conn., were close friends, and collaborated on a book.

Warner, who was born in Plainfield, Mass., in 1829 and died in Hartford in 1900, was a sort of Great Cham of polite letters near the turn of the century. He wrote a large number of books, some of them still resisting the dust bins of literature but, by one of those strange quirks of fate, he is best known, or would be best known if the record of American literature had not somehow become cockeyed, through one sentence of eleven words.

Warner worked up a considerable reputation as an author, editor, critic, traveler, and homespun philosopher, first coming into literary notice with a book *My Summer in a Garden* (1870), made up of articles originally contributed to the Hartford *Courant*. A critic proclaimed that it "placed Mr. Warner in the front rank of American humorists."

It, as well as *Back-Log Studies* (1872); *Being a Boy* (1877); and a handful of others, are read occasionally today.

The famous weather remark was in an editorial Warner wrote for *The Courant* about 1890.

In Burton Stevenson's *Home Book of Quotations*, the despairing cry of an editor of *The Courant* is quoted:

"I guess it's no use; they still believe Mark Twain said it, despite all my assurances that it was Warner."

If you should feel chagrined that you didn't know the source of the quotation then you can move over with H. L. Mencken who reproduced it in his monumental *A New Dictionary of Quotations* (1942), followed by this gloss: "Author unidentified; commonly ascribed to S. L. Clemens (Mark Twain) but not found in his published works."

Paging Charles Dudley Warner

Likewise, you are akin with one of the best informed men on American letters. Asked today if he could explain why Warner had been deprived of his due credit, he promptly confessed he didn't even know Warner was the author.

The only Twain remark about the weather that has got into the anthologies and quotation books is this:

"There is a sumptuous variety about New England weather that compels the stranger's admiration — and regret. . . . In the Spring I have counted one hundred and thirty-six different kinds of weather inside of twenty-four hours."

Mark tossed that one off in a speech at a dinner of the New England Society in New York in 1876.

Twain's collaboration with Warner on a novel *The Gilded Age,* published in 1874, is called by biographer Albert Bigelow Paine a perfectly natural development since both men were established authors, friends and neighbors in Hartford. The partnership was the result of a dinner table conversation between the two families.

As this collaboration probably is Warner's second best toehold on fame, here's how it came about:

"Clemens had the beginning of a story in his mind, but had been unwilling to undertake an extended work of fiction alone," Paine writes. He welcomed only too eagerly, therefore, the proposition of joint authorship. The idea appealed to Warner, and there was no delay in the beginning.

In a letter to the Editor of the New York *Daily Graphic,* on April 17, 1873, Twain said:

"During the last two months my next-door neighbor, Chas. Dudley Warner, has dropped his 'Back-Log Studies,' and he and I have written a bulky novel in partnership. He has worked up the fiction and I have turned in the facts. I consider it one of the most astonishing novels that ever was written. Night after night I sit up reading it over and over again and crying. It will be published early in the fall, with plenty of pictures. Do you consider this an advertisement? — and if so, do you charge for such things, and when a man is your friend and an orphan?"

In spite of Mark's statement, the book was only a minor success, although a play made from it was quite popular.

Occasionally another well known statement is attributed to Twain:

"What this country really needs is a good five-cent cigar."

More people, however, know that the father of that one was the late Vice President Thomas R. Marshall.* He said it while presiding over the United States Senate during a debate on the needs of the country.

* On August 2, 1948, Representative John W. McCormack of Massachusetts went Tom Marshall one better. He said what the country needs is a good seven-cent nickel, and he introduced a bill into Congress to create such a coin. "The five-cent nickel just isn't what it used to be," he declared. "At present price levels, it's a coin that can't do the work it's supposed to do."

WHODUNIT?

. . . one vote for Thomas Bailey Aldrich

From a drawing by HENRY BARROW

THE WEATHER AGAIN

May 8, 1948

EVERYBODY is talking about the weather again. Therefore it is appropriate to talk about the man who once made a famous remark about the weather.

Again, you say? Wasn't that business disposed of when the crown was snatched from the head of Mark Twain and placed on the brow of Charles Dudley Warner?

Well, not exactly. That famous phrase: "everybody talks about the weather but nobody does anything about it" has more lives than the proverbial cat. The whole controversy as to authorship has been stirred up again by a newly published book.

I'm not backing down on Warner. There is plenty of circumstantial evidence that the one-time editorial writer for the Hartford *Courant* produced it around 1890. Certainly, nobody has turned up any convincing evidence that he didn't. And those who still have an open mind on Mark Twain have no direct evidence for their hero, either.

Likely the matter never will be settled to everybody's satisfaction until someone puts the finger on the actual quotation, properly attributed, in the pages of *The Courant*. Past searchers (including *Courant* checkers) have failed to pan any gold, but the task is to be tackled again some day.

One of the citations in favor of Warner is in Burton Stevenson's *Home Book of Quotations* (originally published in 1934). Stevenson quotes this despairing cry of an editor of *The Courant*:

"I guess it's no use; they still believe Mark Twain said it, despite all my assurances that it was Warner."

In the recently published *Mark Twain at Your Fingertips* (Beechhurst Press), the quotation again is attributed to Mark. The editor, Caroline Thomas Harnsberger, gives as her authority a story on page 322 of Robert Underwood Johnson's *Remembered Yesterdays* (1923).

This searcher immediately tackled page 322 of the Johnson opus. He found this:

"Nor have I ever seen in print Mark's saying about the weather. 'We all grumble about the weather, but' (dramatic pause) '—but—but nothing is *done* about it.' He was a master in the piquant use of the pause at the right moment."

Now, this is an exasperating reference. For one thing the quotation varies to a considerable extent from the generally accepted version and the one that Mrs. Harnsberger prints in her book.

More confusing, however, is that fact that Johnson does not make clear whether he actually heard Mark make the weather statement, or whether he simply is repeating an anecdote from another source. For almost every other story in his chapter on Twain Johnson says outright that he was with the author and heard him directly. But on this vital story he just leaves the attribution in the air. In a poetic haze let us say (Johnson was a poet).

Some reviewers of Mrs. Harnsberger's book particularly mentioned the weather story. One was a writer who signs himself "Bookwright" in the New York *Herald Tribune*. Later, "Bookwright" came up with this paragraph:

"In my note on Caroline Thomas Harnsberger's *Mark Twain at Your Fingertips* I accepted Mrs. Harnsberger's ascription to Mark Twain of the famous saying that 'everybody talks about the weather but nobody does anything about it.' Mrs. Harnsberger gives as her authority Robert Underwood Johnson's *Remembered Yesterdays*. But two correspondents have written that the remark should be ascribed to Thomas Bailey Aldrich or to Charles Dudley Warner. Warner is said by Burton Egbert Stevenson to have written it in an editorial for the Hartford *Courant* 'about 1890.' Why does not some enterprising reporter go through the files of that excellent newspaper and either discover the original quotation or else prove it is not there?"

What's this, another entry for the honors? Yes, Thomas Bailey

Aldrich, another poet, has at least one champion. As if the situation wasn't complicated enough as it is!

But, answering Bookwright about research on the files of *The Courant* — that has been done. This was learned when I put the whole controversy before George Hiram Brownell of Elkhorn, Wis., Director of Research for the "Mark Twain Research Foundation," and George E. Stansfield, managing editor of *The Courant*.

Brownell, who is the leading bibliographical scholar on Twain's writings, said:

"As to the Twain weather gag, I am going to keep an open mind on the question as to whether Warner or Twain is the author.

"The first searcher I hired was told to examine the files of *The Courant*, both news columns and editorial columns of circa 1890. The next searcher was told to examine the editorial columns only. Neither found anything — total cost in cash out of my pocket was $23.

"Their search covered a six months' period preceding and following the year 1890. What should be done — and will be done by the Foundation if finances permit, is to continue the search for two or three years each side of 1890. In fact, the search, if not then successful, should be extended to cover the entire period of Warner's editorship.

"And while that search is being made, it might as well be extended to cover everything by and about Twain that appeared in *The Courant* from 1867 to the time of Twain's death and even later. Thar's gold in that *Courant* that nobody seems to have taken the trouble to dig out."

While Mr. Stansfield said *The Courant's* own search had not been productive, the attribution of the remark to Warner has been of long standing in *The Courant* office.

The late Charles Hopkins Clark, who was editor of *The Courant* for many years, was cited by Stansfield as one staunch authority for Warner's side.

The fact remains, however, that the famous words are not to be found in the presently known writings of either author.

The Weather Again

Since Warner and Twain were close friends and neighbors and collaborated on one book, it may turn out that they collaborated on these eleven words.

That, I think, would satisfy everybody.

DEPARTMENT OF UTTER CONFUSION

In the meantime (to carry on the story) "Bookwright" had done a bit of checking of his own with *The Courant*. This note appeared over his signature in the *Herald Tribune* weekly book review on May 23, 1948:

A letter from Herbert Brucker, editor of "The Hartford Courant," comes as near to furnishing a document on the remark about the weather ascribed to Mark Twain as anything I have seen. Mr. Brucker says enterprising reporters and other researchers have gone through the "Courant" files and have come up with nothing "more final than an editorial published on August 24, 1897. This editorial began with the sentence, 'A well known American writer said once that, while everybody talked about the weather, nobody seemed to do anything about it.' Charles Dudley Warner was writing editorials in 'The Courant' at that time. But we have no records proving that he wrote this specific editorial, nor do we know whether the other writer to whom he refers actually existed, or whether it was just a dodge to introduce the idea." There, for the present, the case stands.

I thought that would be the end of the matter so far as I was concerned, so I put away my files and prepared to forget about the subject. But you don't just kiss things off that easy.

In July 1948 an advance copy of Burton Stevenson's new *Home Book of Proverbs* reached the office. Just out of curiosity I looked up the weather remark again and found that something had been added. It was the statement: "See editorial by M. S. Sherman in *The Courant*, January 5, 1945."

So I wrote to Managing Editor Stansfield asking if he could

furnish me a copy of the editorial — but unfortunately I gave the date as 1948 instead of 1945. Stansfield replied:

"I am enclosing to you a copy of an editorial which was written by Mr. M. S. Sherman on February 6, 1947. Mr. Sherman, as you know, died in June of that year.

"No editorial has appeared in *The Courant* on this subject under date of January 5, 1948, so it occurred to me that this is possibly the editorial you have in mind."

The editorial reads:

GIVE WARNER THE CREDIT

We never expect that it can be lived down, but let it once more be said that it was Charles Dudley Warner, and nobody else, who made the often-quoted quip, "Everybody talks about the weather, but nobody does anything about it." Mr. Warner was associate editor of The Courant at the time he made the comment, which was almost instantly taken up by newspapers generally and credited to Mark Twain, an intimate friend of Warner.

At various times during his editorship of The Courant, Charles Hopkins Clark, who personally knew all the circumstances attending the quotation, sought to set the matter right, but with little avail. From that day to this the quip has been repeatedly credited to Mark Twain.

The present editor of The Courant has had considerable correspondence with many persons throughout the country on the subject, and he succeeded in convincing Mr. Burton Stevenson, author of the "Home Book of Quotations," that Warner was entitled to all the credit for his sage observation about the weather, particularly the New England weather, with which he was most familiar.

Of this particular brand of weather it was Mark Twain who said, "If you don't like what you've got, wait a minute." He also said, "There is a sumptuous variety about New England weather that compels the stranger's admiration — and regret. . . . In the Spring I have counted 136 different kinds of weather inside of twenty-four hours." But let us repeat by way of further emphasis that it was Warner who said, "Everybody talks about the weather but nobody does anything about it."

The Weather Again

It was now evident to me that a conspiracy of some kind was afoot to prevent getting at what may be the solution. Sadly I informed Stansfield of my error in the date, and said I presumed that the 1945 editorial was along the same line as the 1947 printing.

In resignation I also told Stansfield that just that morning I again had heard the radio attribute the remark to Mark Twain. It was a program for an air cooling device, and the announcer said emphatically that his company really could do something about the weather.

THE MYSTERY OF
THE CARDBOARD HAT BOX

August 16, 1947

TANTALIZING NEWS of the discovery of unpublished Sherlock Holmes stories has been coming from London for several years.

A current cable reveals that Adrian Conan Doyle, son of Sir Arthur, has found at least two additional items concerning the angular sleuth among the late writer's papers.

The only trouble, from the standpoint of Sherlock Holmes enthusiasts in the United States, is that nothing ever seems to materialize from these announcements.

Holmes fanatics got their first shot in the arm through word in 1942 that a tale of some 7000 words had just come to light. The Doyle estate, however, held at that time that this number was one of Sir Arthur's poorer efforts and that the author's reputation would suffer if it were given to the world.

A considerable clamor was raised and for a time it appeared that the estate would quickly relent to permit the story — "The Man Who Was Wanted" — to be released, at least for private circulation among the more ardent worshippers at the Sherlockian shrine.

That's as far as it went, however, for years. What next happened was that a few hundred words of the yarn were printed in Hesketh Pearson's biography of Sir Arthur in 1943 and reprinted on this side of the Atlantic in a brochure *A Baker Street Four-Wheeler* the following year. The latter item, edited by Edgar W. Smith, a General Motors executive and High Priest of all Sherlock Holmes idolaters, had only a limited circulation among members of the Baker Street Irregulars.

[69]

The Mystery of the Cardboard Hat Box

Thus, with the Sherlockian world still waiting * for the complete story, the announcement of the new find is not only tantalizing but exasperating as well to devotees.

The recent word from London was that the new material had turned up in an old cardboard hat box stored in a country bank.

Adrian Conan Doyle said the manuscripts included an unpublished one-act play, "The Crown and Diamond — An Evening with Sherlock Holmes," and some notes called "Some Personalia About Mr. Sherlock Holmes."

"There is no doubt 'The Crown and Diamond' is an unpublished play by Sir Arthur." Doyle said. "From examinations of his writing and the text of the play itself I should say it was written about the time of *The Return of Sherlock Holmes* — in the early 1900s."

It was written in a little exercise book.

Doyle said the find was made when he, his brother and sister went to the bank at Crowborough, Sussex, to remove some papers which their father had stored there in 1922, eight years before his death.

As usual, there was no announcement whether or when the material would be made public.

The situation surrounding the earlier discovered story, "The Man Who Was Wanted," was summed up in Edgar Smith's introduction to the fragment printed in *A Baker Street Four-Wheeler*:

---

* The complete story finally saw the light of day in the August 1948 *Cosmopolitan*. While this fact dates some of the above details, I have let them run along anyway for the sake of chronology. The BSI folks still are steamed up and the best they will allow is that "The Man Who Was Wanted" is nothing more than a pastiche.

Vincent Starrett, in his "Books Alive" column in the Chicago *Sunday Tribune* for August 15, 1948, had this to say of the tale:

"It is not a bad story, but one understands why Sir Arthur laid it aside. No doubt he intended to return to it some day, to give it the extra vitality, the special flavor, that would bring it to satisfying stature among the other adventures. As it stands, the tale lacks incident and pace; but the idea is ingenious, and there are passages that remind one of some of the best episodes in the saga; in particular the early paragraphs of banter between the detective and Dr. Watson, involving a spot of typical Holmesian deduction."

The Mystery of the Cardboard Hat Box

"First word of the existence of an unpublished manuscript from the pen of John H. Watson, M.D., came to the United States on July 15, 1942, when Mr. P. M. Stone of Boston, received from his friend Bertram Rota of Bodley House, London, a copy of The London *Star* of June 13th. A special writer mentioned rather casually in his column that day the discovery by Mr. Hesketh Pearson of the text of a new Sherlock Holmes story among the papers of the late Sir Arthur Conan Doyle, whose biography Pearson was then engaged in writing. Sir Arthur, who acted during his lifetime as Dr. Watson's literary agent (this is a whimsy nourished by the BSI), had evidently felt the tale to be inferior in quality, and had refused to permit its publication."

Pearson's opinion was that the opening scenes of the story in Holmes' quarters were "quite as good as anything that Conan Doyle did, but the plot is weak."

Here is how Doyle — or shall we say Watson — opened the tale:

"One of my best patients was in a very critical state at the time, and it was not until August was gone that he passed the crisis and began to recover. Feeling then that I could leave my practice with a good conscience in the hands of a locum tenens, I began to wonder where and how I should best find the rest and change I needed.

"Almost at once the idea came to my mind that I would hunt up my old friend Sherlock Holmes, whom I had seen nothing of for several months. Within half an hour of coming to this resolution I was standing in the doorway of the familiar old room in Baker Street.

"Holmes was stretched on the couch with his back towards me, the familiar dressing gown and old briar pipe as much in evidence as of yore.

" 'Come in, Watson,' he cried cheerily, without glancing around. 'Come in and tell me what good winds blow you here.' "

From there on for the next few hundred words the tale has the authentic Sherlockian ring.

While the Baker Street Irregulars and its scion societies have been signally unsuccessful in getting new material released they have attracted considerable attention in recent years in their devotion to the master and the propagation of his virtues.

The parent body was founded in New York in 1934 by a band of hot-shot literary figures, but the organization languished until 1940 when "Buttons" (Secretary) Smith took over. Since then branches have sprung up all over the country, ranging from a hefty aggregation, "The Hounds of the Baskerville," in Chicago to "The Solitary Cyclist," composed of the one and only member in Washington, D.C. — Helene Yuhasova.

Here are some of the other scion societies:

The Six Napoleons of Baltimore. This chapter meets in a restaurant near the grave of Edgar Allan Poe, author of the world's first detective stories.

The Amateur Mendicant Society of Detroit.

The Three Students of Long Island.

The Scandalous Bohemians of Akron, Ohio.

The Five Orange Pips of Westchester County.

The Diogenes Club Beta of Oklahoma.

The Seventeen Steps of Los Angeles.

The Scowrers of San Francisco.

The Speckled Band of Boston. Next to the Baker Street Irregulars this is the oldest of the American societies; and already it has published a book of writings on the canon — *The Second Cab* — and expects to turn out a yearly volume.

The Illustrious Clients of Indianapolis.

Pondicherry Lodge of Springfield, Illinois.

The Wisteria Lodge of Confederates of the Eastern Deep South, with headquarters in Pine Bluff, N.C.

This rash of junior societies has jumped the border into Canada where the Canadian Baskervilles hold forth in Hamilton, Ontario.

As a result of all this activity, the lore of Sherlock Holmes has grown at a prodigious pace. Most of the society members are professional or amateur authors and it appears that practically everybody wants to take a slash at an essay, poem or book.

The Irregulars put out a quarterly journal devoted entirely to

Sherlock and each of the scion societies has some publication plan in the works.

Sir Arthur would be mightily surprised at all this to-do in behalf of a character he did not particularly care for.

By CHARLES HONCE

THIS is a map you have never seen before and the like of which you may never see again.

At first glance it appears to be a map of Europe before World War I. A closer scrutiny will show that it is no such thing. Rather, it is a chart of a Never-Never land—a place of romance and wizardry—although many people will claim that it is just as real as any map ever concocted.

In brief, this is the Europe in which Sherlock Holmes operated in a day when about the

SCENES IN THE HOLMES SAGA

1 MADRID The Adventure of the Norwood Builder

2 BORDEAUX A Case of Identity

3 GRENOBLE The Adventure of the Empty House.

4 REICHENBACH. The Final Problem.

5 PARIS. The Adventure of the Illustrious Client.

6 FRANKFORT A Study in Scarlet.

7 "BOHEMIA." A Scandal in Bohemia.

8 AUSTRIA-HUNGARY His Last Bow.

9 BERLIN. His Last Bow.

10 WARSAW A Scandal in Bohemia.

11 SWEDEN. The Valley of Fear.

A LAND OF FAR AWAY

From an Associated Press "Background Map"
Cartography by Dr. Julian Wolff

A BAKER STREET VIEW
OF EUROPE

February 28, 1948

THIS is a map you have never seen before and the like of which you
may never see again.

At first glance it appears to be a map of Europe before World
War I. A closer scrutiny will show that it is no such thing. Rather,
it is a chart of a Never-Never land — a place of romance and
wizardry — although many people will claim that it is just as real as
any map ever concocted.

In brief, this is the Europe in which Sherlock Holmes operated
in a day when about the only problems facing the continent had to
do with a stolen gem or a sedate scandal in high places. There
probably is a sufficient if not vitally compelling reason for reproducing it today in place of the inevitable map bearing tidings of
wars, iron curtains, and crises. That reason is that this, by a little
stretch of the imagination, can be considered an anniversary — a
Sherlock Holmes Birthday anniversary, and time for a moment of
nostalgia.

It happens that Sherlock Holmes was born (mentally if not
physically) 61 years ago. At least it was in 1887 that Sir Arthur
Conan Doyle began weaving his tales of the famous sleuth.

Assuming that Sherlock was reasonably mature at the time, he
would be somewhere in the middle nineties today. An important
thing to bear in mind is that he still is alive. He hasn't been heard

[77]

from lately and the man who recorded his adventures is no more. But Holmes, at last reports, was tending his bees on a farm in Sussex, and there is no reason to believe that he isn't there still. He couldn't have returned to his old home at 221-B Baker Street, London, as a bomb took care of that address during the German blitz. And certainly his name has never appeared on the obituary page of the London *Times*.

Therefore, it may be surmised that this map eventually may catch his eye and provide a reminder of the famous cases he solved in a day when the world was a million or so years younger and simpler.

Dr. Julian Wolff of New York made the map. He also has turned out several others spotting the adventures of Sherlock around the known world, and not overlooking the American episodes. Likewise, he is the author of a pamphlet "A Catalogue of 221-B Culture" and other Sherlockian numbers, indicating the extent of his interest in the Old Master.

Dr. Wolff says he has had "a lot of fun" turning out his charts and maps, and while it has been a labor of love he also has found a nostalgic satisfaction in the business.

"It is only too true that in these times the publication of a map only serves to indicate the location of a new area where war or peace has broken out," he says. "Just by being different and by affording some refuge from these realities, and by reminding us of the real good old days when it was practical to draw boundaries in indelible ink, this map justifies its existence.

"Of course, true Sherlockians will find another reason for the map. For those armchair investigators who resemble Mycroft rather than Sherlock and require that the mountain come to Mohammed, it is of real service. It indicates the locations of many places which are unknown to Messrs. Rand and McNally as well as all their colleagues, although they are extremely interesting to the numerous friends of Sherlock Holmes and Dr. Watson.

"Besides, it helps keep track of the old names which seem to be changing as completely as the old boundaries. Certainly Bohemia is preferable to Czechoslovakia. And as for a choice between St. Petersburg and Leningrad!

"Moreover the useful information included on the map may even serve as a reminder of the interesting items found in the works of the old cartographers who made map-making the art that it used to be, and no longer is."

Now let's get back to the actual map. Those shields along the bottom are keys to some of Holmes' outstanding adventures. One of the best known is "A Scandal in Bohemia" — recorded in the first of the short stories and the one that introduced "THE Woman"— Irene Adler. Irene is the number one toast of the Baker Street Irregulars.

The place names and the notes will be well known to all Sherlock Holmes fans, who seem to grow in numbers yearly under the energetic and sometimes fanatic promotion of the Irregulars.

Next, cast your eye on Switzerland with its "X" at Reichenbach marking the "spot where the body was not found."

This is a red-flag reminder for any Sherlock Holmes addict since it is the place where Doyle once tried to kill off his detective. In spite of the fact that the author ingeniously returned Holmes to circulation, after considerable public clamor, Sherlock's fans still haven't forgiven Sir Arthur.

"It is, indeed, a fearful place," recorded Watson in "The Final Problem," referring to the falls of Reichenbach. "The torrent, swollen by the melting snow, plunges into a tremendous abyss."

And it was into that abyss, Watson surmised, that Holmes reeled to his death, locked in the arms of that "Napoleon of crime," Professor Moriarty.

"Any attempt at recovering the bodies was absolutely hopeless," Watson continued. But he was wrong — sadly wrong, as he was on so many other occasions and as all proper stooges have been through the ages.

Holmes did return to many more adventures, and even did the British Government a smart turn in World War One.

He's always been known to turn up in a pinch. And even though he is in his nineties today that doesn't mean that he's entirely washed up. Can it be possible that maybe we again will hear that stirring call to action?

"Come Watson, come! The game is afoot!"

SHERLOCK HOLMES ON THE AIR

All during the war, and since, The Associated Press has turned out a weekly "Background Map," with the text and chart based on some important event in the week's news. I wondered if something a little lighter could be included without bringing down the world.

So I produced the above piece based on Dr. Wolff's map and sent it on its way. I expected the whimsy might rile some serious minded editors — but nothing happened.

The story even got on the radio. Tom O'Neil, Associated Press Radio News Editor, ground out a little dramatic sketch for "Side Street America," a feature on the AP radio news wire. His production follows:

NARRATOR: On what may be regarded as the birthday of the great detective, Sherlock Holmes, something has been done about it. It was 61 years ago that the first story about the famous sleuth unravelling a mystery came from the pen of Arthur Conan Doyle. Now the Baker Street Irregulars have a map out about his exploits. These Irregulars meet when the spirit moves and in fantasy consider what Sherlock would do about problems of the moment. Why a map? Let Charles Honce (Hawnss) of New York, one of the Irregulars, explain:

VOICE: At first glance it appears to be a map of Europe before World War One. A closer scrutiny will show it's no such thing. Rather, it's a chart of Never-Never land, a place of Romance and wizardry, although many people will claim it is just as real as any map ever concocted.

NARRATOR: The map shows the scene of every adventure of Sherlock Holmes, A Study in Scarlet, A Scandal in Bohemia, and the like. It includes Reichenbach, where Doctor Watson surmised that Holmes reeled to his death locked in the arms of that Napoleon of crime, Professor

Moriarty. But Watson was all wrong, according to the spokesman of the Baker Street Irregulars.

VOICE: Holmes did return to many more adventures. He's always been known to turn up in a pinch.

NARRATOR: He could not have returned to his old home at 221-B Baker Street, London. A bomb took care of that address during the blitz. But the Irregulars are die-hards.

VOICE: Holmes hasn't been heard from lately and the man who recorded his adventures is no more. But Holmes, at last reports, was tending his bees on a farm in Sussex and there's no reason to believe he isn't there still.

MY FIRST MEETING WITH
SHERLOCK HOLMES *

(BEN ABRAMSON, deputizing for Edgar W. Smith, who was on one of those mysterious trips to Washington, phoned me at noon one day recently and said: "We're going to have a department in the new magazine called 'My First Meeting With Sherlock Holmes,' and we want you to start it off. Can we have your copy by 3 P.M. today?" I answered Nay on two counts; first, I had a bit of office work to attend to and then, again, my recollection of my introduction to Sherlock was hazy at best, far back in the century, absolutely normal and completely lacking in public interest. "However," I said, with some impish perversity, "I'm prepared tonight to atomize the sacred tradition by knocking off a piece on 'Why I am Not a Sherlock Holmes Collector.'" Then Ben said Nay, somewhat aghast. I rather liked the idea, however; said I'd do it anyway and that he and Smith could decide whether they wanted to run it. If they do, and if in the meantime they don't flag someone else for a try on the "My First Meeting" theme, I'll try to make this qualify in a limited way by saying that I find in my library a book called *Tales of Sherlock Holmes*, inscribed "Xmas 1910 From Mama to Charlie." It is a miscellaneous collection of the long and short stories. I am sure, however, that I read all the Sherlock Holmes stories the Keokuk Public Library possessed some years earlier. Very probably I started around 1906, at which time I was ten years old, so that my acquaintance with the master is of fairly long standing. The "Tales" happens to be the first Sherlock Holmes

* From Volume 1, Number 1 of the *Baker Street Journal*, January 1946.

book that went into my personal library. It has had an honored place on my shelves for thirty-five years, and naturally it will be there so long as I live. Now for my heretical document:)

❀   ❀   ❀

H. L. Mencken wrote an Introduction for a recent book of mine — a book about books — and I titled his piece "Why I am Not a Book Collector." He had suggested he might turn out his overture on that theme, but when the actual article arrived and I had read it I immediately wrote him that so far as I could tell his description of his book collecting activities just about paralleled the experience of any other collector I had known.

"About the only difference," I told him, "is that you are on your third collection while the average book collector still is struggling with his first or second efforts."

Mencken came back with this: "What you say really astonishes me. I have never thought of myself as a book collector."

Maybe I'm in the same boat regarding Sherlock Holmes. Let's set down the record and see what happens.

No first edition of any Sherlock Holmes book is to be found on my shelves. I do not consciously collect Sherlockiana, although in the normal course of acquiring things and knowing people I have accumulated a basketful of items which are scattered in job lots around the house.

My grade would be pretty awful on any Sherlock Holmes quiz, and I am the perpetual dunce at any gathering of the Baker Street Irregulars. In fact, I can't even understand much of the erudite and esotoric things those Sherlock Holmes pundits write about their favorite god. In other words, I am just about a complete blank in the realm of the higher criticism.

And yet, in spite of this negative and embarrassing record, somehow or other I have acquired a glowing reputation as a Sherlock Holmes specialist; and hardly any project involving the sleuth germinates without my name being in, on or connected with it. Even complete strangers write to me as an oracle on the subject,

and collectors ask with bated breath to see the nuggets they presume I am hoarding behind lock and key.

Not that I am a complete washout on the theme. The fact is that Sherlock Holmes is one of my favorites and has been since my early reading days. I read the early stories time and again in that early period, and I grabbed all of the later ones as they came out. And, eventually, I acquired for my library all of the Sherlock Holmes numbers, but in miscellaneous format indeed. (Incidentally, it is rather hard to get together the nine volumes housing the original Watson *opera*; if you don't believe it, go out and try. I'm not referring to omnibus books, but to contemporary appearances [even if not first editions] containing contemporary illustrations.)

My copy of *The Hound of the Baskervilles* has lost its back strip and the other books are getting to be a pretty mouldy lot. But, nevertheless, I have them all, and, occasionally, I do read a story.

But I still can't answer an I.Q. test of any complexity on the sacred writings and a Morley crossword puzzle, so far as I am concerned, is something out of Sanskrit. There simply is no "how many angels can stand on a pinpoint?" in my relations with the master.

Therefore, I presume that the singular notice that has come to me as a result of my rather, shall I say, normal Sherlock Holmes interest has been because of the power of the press. Which means that since 1934, when I wrote a news story on the first meeting of the Baker Street Irregulars (to which I was not invited) I have turned out a score or two of articles on the Old Gentleman, mostly news stories, which reached an audience of many millions of readers and thus helped catapult me to a totally unearned eminence as a scholar.

What I have written, in newspaper parlance, is the story behind the story. There is nothing deep or footnotey about any of them and they are in meat-and-gravy prose. No one of them foists a wife on Holmes or speculates on a difference in dates involving an adventure in 1887.

I don't know how many wives Watson had, or whether he was

a woman, and I don't care; I don't know what Holmes ate for breakfast or where he went to college, and, again, I don't give a damn. I haven't any information on whether Sherlock was an American, or whether, on the other hand, he was really the King of Bohemia — and I am still happy.

Let others delve into the higher mysteries, concoct coats of arms, locate second wounds, check how many motets the sleuth transcribed, and determine that Holmes and Watson were in three places at the same time on the foggy morning of April 7, 1890. I'll stick to my childish stories — most of them right out of the cranium; and I'll continue to like the Sherlock Holmes tales just as they are — minus the modern gadgets.

Well, that's the story. In spite of this extremely brassy reputation of mine, I just don't seem to belong in the august company of these Sherlockian Grand Lamas . . .

I've just reread the above . . .
Move over, Mencken!

      ✿   ✿   ✿

(A vaguely stirring memory sends me to a closet where the sentimentalities of my youth are hidden. Yes, there they are — two three-act playlets I wrote about Sherlock Holmes and printed in my High School magazine in 1912. I had forgotten them until this very moment. Well, whaddaya know!)

GOING, GOING, GONE!*

IF YOU will be patient this eventually will get around to Sherlock Holmes. But I must lead up to it gradually.

First, it is necessary to record that a book I privately distributed for Christmas 1945 included a chapter called "Titles For Sale."

In spite of the fact that the production housed a baker's dozen pieces on Sherlock, that little number on titles drummed up the most comment.

In it I set down a long list of imaginary book labels — seductive under tongue and eye — I had dreamed up and preserved over the years.

Among those who reacted was H. L. Mencken.

He wrote me (December 28, 1945):

". . . I read with especial amusement your proposed titles for books. I enclose a couple of them that have occurred to me under the influence of Christmas cheer":

THE CHIEF JUSTICE'S REVENGE

WIVES GALORE

LET US PRAY

TEN THOUSAND DAMNS

THE ENCHANTED HORSE AND BUGGY

GOING, GOING, GONE!

THE GUYASCUTIS

DOWN THE CHUTE

THE MIDNIGHT GUITAR

A SENATOR AT BAY

SPECIES OF FEMALES

THE THREE ARCHDEACONS

MAKE MINE BOURBON

FAIR BUT NOT FAT

OH, YES

* Written in March 1946 for the *Baker Street Journal*. It didn't make the grade.

Going, Going, Gone!

That's a sweet list, and I relish particularly THE CHIEF JUSTICE'S REVENGE, A SENATOR AT BAY, and THE THREE ARCHDEACONS.

But the tag that brought a real nostalgic twinge was:

GOING, GOING, GONE!

That's because it sent me back to a boyhood in Keokuk, Iowa.

My father was a barber and it was a great occasion in my life when I was permitted quietly to sit in the back of his shop and watch the fascinating happenings in such ultra-sophisticated surroundings.

Let's pick a date in 1908 and enter.

On the wall is a placard with a legend well known in those days:

GOING, GOING, GONE!

It advertised, as oldsters will recall, a hair tonic known as Herpicide. It pictured a lugubrious youth, in three poses, running a comb through his hair and finding on the third operation that he was totally bald.

But, at the same time, on the Victorian table holding the *Police Gazette* and other publications of the period, was a copy of *Collier's*.

A boy, tiring of the Herpicide ad and its dismal moral "too late for Herpicide," thumbed through the magazine and breathlessly discovered that it was all about Sherlock Holmes.

It was the issue of August 15, 1908 — the "Sherlock Holmes Number" — and now a collector's item. It contained (an adult reinvestigation reveals) such items as Carolyn Wells' "Ballade of Baker Street"; a long article on "Sherlock Holmes and His Creator," by Arthur Bartlett Maurice; the first American appearance of "The Singular Experience of Mr. J. Scott Eccles," and other absorbing material. The cover, by Frederic Dorr Steele, is to my thinking the finest Sherlock portrait ever turned out by the artist.

But, in 1908 a youth was confused. He had believed that Sherlock Holmes was a fictional character. And yet, here in *Collier's,* the sleuth seemingly came true to life. Or at least the dividing line

between dream and reality was too finely drawn for a bewildered kid.

He asked many persons what was the answer, but no one could tell him precisely.

He still is confused.

He still can't be sure whether Sherlock is the real McCoy or an impostor.

❧   ❧   ❧

Other readers also sent me in suggestions for titles and I have piled up a few new ones myself. Here's a second harvest:

> A SKY FULL OF MOONS
> MORNING-GO-ROUND (*heard on the radio*)
> ONCE UPON A MOON
> THE ANGEL OF THE DARKER DREAM
> SUMMER SEAS
> INDOLENT DREAMS
> WALTZ IN DREAM TIME
> MAY I SPEAK!
> IT WON'T BE LONG
> NOW YOU LISTEN TO ME!
> ORCHIDS AT NOON
> ALL THE DEAD DAY
> A SUMMER WITH A THOUSAND JULYS
> (*a line from a popular song*)
> SQUARE CHECKERS
> SOMEDAY AFTERNOON
> FROM BACH TO BE-BOP
> VIRGINS AND CENTAURS

"We think he's going to be an anthologist"

A cartoon by Carl Rose *from "One Dozen Roses"*

A MAN WHO LOVED BOOKS

THE TOP MAN of the Kingdom of Books is dead.

Holbrook Jackson, who wrote that monumental tome *The Anatomy of Bibliomania* (1930), cashed in his books at Bournemouth, Hampshire, England on June 16, 1948 at the age of 73.

I never met this Titan but I corresponded with him over a period of years. One of my real literary treasures is a remark he made about my writing style; it was the rosiest compliment that ever fell my way.

Our correspondence developed in a curious way. I had known and admired Jackson's writings for many years and I assumed that he turned out his erudite numbers in some dream tower far from the haunts of men.

Then I learned through a mutual friend that actually Jackson earned his bread and Elzevirs as editorial director of The National Trade Press in London which turned out such down to earth magazines as *The Draper's Organiser, The Footwear Organiser, The Furnishing Trades' Organiser* and a dozen other trade and technical journals.

On the other hand, the mutual friend who knew Jackson because he was in the trade press field on this side of the Atlantic, learned for the first time from me of Jackson's unique place in the world of books.

Jackson's bibliography is a long one but the main gem always will be the *Anatomy.* I wouldn't advise anyone to dive into it without prayer and meditation. John Carter, in his *Taste and Technique in Book Collecting* (1948), says it is "a book as rich in plums (and as indigestible in large helpings) as a Christmas pudding." The *Anatomy* actually is a trilogy. When *The Fear of Books* was published in 1932 Jackson wrote "This book is complete in itself, but I like to think of it as a part of its predecessor, *The Anatomy of*

Bibliomania." Then, in 1947, came *The Reading of Books.* It carried on the tradition.

Jackson wrote these books in a leisurely, purposely archaic style. So don't try to gallop through them. Sit back and relax, follow Carter's advice and take a mouthful at a time.

Since Mr. Jackson's letters have given me so much pleasure, I append them here:

1 Winterstoke Gardens Mill Hill London N.W. 7
18:ii:41

My dear Mr. Honce — Ever since Everit Terhune reported a friendly remark made by you about my books I have been waiting in vain for an occasion to write to you — and now you have given me the best of openings — your book of essays reached me yesterday and after initial greetings in the form of pattings and featherings and other evidences of bibliographic glee — not excluding dippings! I brought the graceful volume home for more intimate acquaintance at the fireside. As I put my paper-knife into action and began to listen to its whispering passage through the beautifully flexible paper — the syrens began to howl their too familiar Valkyrie Chorus and the A.A. guns sent up their defiance to the night raiders — but your book beat the raid which lasted three-and-a-half hours and later it ousted Anthony Trollope's *Little House at Allington* which is my present bed-book. So you can see that I owe you my thanks. I have now read through the whole book and re-read several passages — with continuous enjoyment and many additions to my knowledge of books — particularly the lighter and more exciting kinds of fiction. The idea of collecting and studying bibliographically popular and often ephemeral books is excellent — I think it began in the USA although some have adventured in those difficult realms over here, notably Michael Sadleir who made a study of "yellow backs" and "railway novels." Generally collectors lack courage to face anything but a classic — thus *Robinson Crusoe* is sky rocketed and *The Daybourne* neglected — as I grow older I find memories of the bookish enthusiasms of my very early days crowding my mind and I have had to resist the temptation to go out on the trail of the *Swiss Family Robinson* or *Helen's Babies* or *Daddy Darwin's Dovecot!* But I am perhaps too old to be decoyed from my own hunting grounds which are pleasant little spots not unconnected with Joseph Glanvill, Robert Burton, and Sir Henry Wotton — most of the treasures, alas! are packed away in a concrete shelter in the hope that they will escape the German bombers who have a genius for destroying books.

Yours very sincerely

HOLBROOK JACKSON

The Athenaeum
Pall Mall S.W. I.
7:iv:42

Dear Mr. Honce — The three books you so kindly sent me for Xmas arrived safely almost three weeks ago. I have read them with enjoyment and benefit. Your bookish 'news stories' wear well and it was an inspiration to reprint them in more permanent form. Even on subjects upon which I am supposed to be expert (Henry Harland for instance) you tell me things I did not know. Julian Hawthorne was little more than the son of his father to me and I am surprised to learn from you that he wrote so much and sometimes so well. I have been *trying* to find a copy of his *Nathaniel Hawthorne and His Wife* without success. It is not in the London Library and I have not yet had time to search the British Museum — where I ought to find it. Your chief revelation however is Vincent Starrett. He is little known over here. I just knew the name and thought it a funny name — and left it at that! Now I am going to read him. He seems to have the right bookish instincts —

Since I last wrote to you our two nations have become united in arms — and alas, in tribulation — but whatever we suffer now cannot alter the happy ending — provided that we all have the guts to stick it and develope intelligence by the way — I am convinced that we have the staying power and can acquire the right technique. We are vexed about Singapore, etc., in England — but not down-hearted. I heard a rumour that you* had joined what corresponds to our Ministry of Information — if so good luck —

Yours sincerely

HOLBROOK JACKSON

* He may have been thinking of Byron Price, who left The Associated Press to become Director of Censorship.

A Man Who Loved Books

1 Winterstoke Gardens Mill Hill London N.W. 7
14:vi:43

My dear Mr. Honce — Some three weeks ago *The Private* [sic] *Papers of a Bibliomaniac* arrived safely and in good condition after what appears to have been a long journey and as I was just leaving London for a brief spell of fresh air and freedom from Air Raid warnings among the Yorkshire dales I took the precious volume with me and was thus able to share your enthusiasms and enjoy your point of view in peace and quietness — and my thanks went out to you after every chapter. Much of your territory is strange to me but none the less interesting, and occasionally I feel more at home as for instance when you handle Mark Twain and Walt Whitman and George Ade and Stephen Crane, and H. L. Mencken of whom I never weary — his *American Language* is a masterly work. Your unconventional way of illustrating the book is an inspiration and a delight — only one thing in the volume gave me an unpleasant knock — at the foot of p. 133 you revealed to me that Vincent Starrett had anticipated me in the title *Bookman's Holiday* which I had used for an anthology* not yet printed — a copy of which I hope to send you under its new name (not yet invented) before many months are passed.

Again thanks

Yours ever

HOLBROOK JACKSON

---

* The book was published in the United States in 1947 as *Bookman's Pleasure*, although it is still referred to as *Bookman's Holiday* in the Preface. This is one of those mysteries that give bibliographers fallen arches.

A Man Who Loved Books

I treasure above all, however, what Jackson said in a letter to his old friend Everit Terhune under date of June 18, 1943:

". . . Charles Honce's latest volume was a long time on the way but eventually reached me safe and sound, and accompanied me a fortnight ago on a brief holiday in the Yorkshire dales, where I read every word, not only with interest but with increasing admiration for Honce's bibliographical sense and his rare gift of being able to expound his enthusiasms in simple, vivid language. He seems to me to have blazed an entirely new trail in bibliographical exposition, and I rejoice that through your kindness my name is on his mailing list. I hope the war will not put an end to his publications. Give him my regards next time you see him and say that a letter thanking him for the book is in the mail."

"YOU CATCH HIM AND WE'LL SEE"

September 13, 1947

NEW ENGLAND's "sea-serpent" is back. He has appeared at one of his favorite haunts — just off the coast of Massachusetts — putting in an appearance after an unexplained absence of ten years.

If he's the same serpent that has been making more or less regular calls at Gloucester or Lynn or Nahant or nearby spots he must be pretty venerable by now since the citizenry of the neighborhood has been pop-eyed by a strange sea visitor since 1815.

This September 1947 report (and bear in mind that the dog days are over and vacation days are on their last dogs) comes from Medford, Massachusetts. A piano-tuner of that estimable town said that he and his two daughters saw "the fifty foot or even longer" monster disporting off Lynn Beach, rolling its barrel-like head and writhing its black coils in and out of the sea.

"Its back showed above the surface at intervals of about every six feet," said the piano-tuner. "I know nobody will believe me but I saw the serpent and my daughter saw it and I'm no fool."

His report follows the classic form where "sea-serpents" are concerned, and before you begin to smile you'd better hear a little of the evidence or, better still, wait until you get a look at your own serpent.

The classic form means (1) that the witness is thoroughly convinced that his eyes did not deceive him, and (2) that through the last one hundred or more years descriptions of these sea creatures from all parts of the world have been virtually identical (though none has ever been caught).

As a writer of sea lore has said: "Most of the witnesses agree on certain outstanding features: it is a long, serpentine creature; it has a series of humps; its head is rather like a horse's; its color is dark on the top and light below; it moves by undulations up and

[99]

down; it appears during the summer months; and unlike the sea-monster it is harmless, for it never actually attacks anybody, even under provocation."

There was one slight variation in this standard description. Old Hiaschuckoluk, reportedly seen by scores of persons off Vancouver Island in 1933, was described as having a face like a camel. Inasmuch as he appeared during prohibition days, the identification was not without its points.

Before getting back to the Massachusetts coast and its more than a century of sea-serpent history, it might be noted that there are two types of visitor out of the mysterious deep. One is the "sea-monster" which from descriptions seems to resemble a giant squid. The sea-monster is reputed to be quite ferocious. The sea-serpent, on the other hand, seems to have a gentle disposition and apparently is content to appear now and then, wave his whiskers, arch his long body, and then take a dive.

The monster has been a familiar figure in the mythology and literature of all peoples who live near the sea. In olden days reputed eye-witnesses stressed its gigantic size and horrific appearance.

In more recent days, however, tellers of sea tales have been more modest about dimensions. For instance, J. G. Lockhart, in his *Mysteries of the Sea* says: "In 1873 two fishermen off the coast of Newfoundland encountered a creature which they described as a gigantic squid. They saw a dark mass floating in the water, and thinking it to be the debris of a wreck, struck at it with a boathook; whereupon it opened out like a huge umbrella, disclosing enormous green eyes and a parrot-like beak, as big as a six-gallon keg. A desperate struggle ensued. The monster grappled the boat with its tentacles, and threatened to drag it, occupants and all, below the surface. At first the men were paralysed with horror; but at length, recovering themselves, they succeeded in severing two of the tentacles, whereupon the monster disappeared. One of the tentacles was brought ashore and carefully examined by Mr. Harvey, a local authority on zoology. Its length was nineteen feet, but a further six feet was destroyed before the measurement was taken, and it was reckoned that nearly ten feet must have remained attached to the body."

The sea-serpent is quite a different proposition.

The giant conger eel (the Vancouver creature was called one by skeptics) often has been mistaken for a sea-serpent, and then there is the veritable serpent of zoology, Ophisura, to be found in the Mediterranean. But the latter is only six feet long while the serpent of legend seldom is under 100 feet. Vancouver's camel-faced creature was described as 80 feet long by 14 witnesses, while a 15th was more conservative with a 40-foot guess.

While there are any number of circumstantial records of sea-monster sightings, science has spoiled romance in most instances by listing water spouts, whales, schools of porpoises in single file, gigantic marine plants and mass psychology as explaining away the stories.*

The first serpent of the 19th century made his appearance off the coast of Scotland in 1808. It was reported seen by many persons, including the parish minister, and was described as 80 feet long.

In the next 30 years an epidemic of sea-serpents was reported from Gloucester and Nahant. One of the earliest, seen in 1815 in Gloucester Bay, was described as 100 feet long, with 40 humps, head like a horse and of a brownish color.

Two years later the Gloucester *Telegram* gave a circumstantial account of a sea-serpent visitation, suggesting that the same creature had returned to the bay:

"On the fourteenth of August the sea-serpent was approached by a boat within 30 feet, and on raising its head above the water was greeted by a volley from the gun of an experienced sportsman. The creature turned directly towards the boat, as if meditating an

---

* When this story was printed in the Omaha *World-Herald*, the Sunday Editor dropped in at this point the following parenthetical note:

> (Sunday editor's note: We favor the conga-line-of-porpoises theory, having frequently seen porpoises on parade in the Pacific. These creatures break water in graceful leaps of identical, or almost identical beats, thus giving the undulating or serpentine effect if the sea is hazy, or if it is near dusk.)

attack, but sank down and soon reappeared at about a hundred yards distance, on the opposite side of the boat."

Nahant reported visitations in 1818 and 1819, while Swampscott came through with the 1820 report. There are various other reports up to 1849 and then a break of 24 years. A commentator notes, however, that very few people, "apart from certain of the population of Gloucester and Nahant, appear to have treated the stories with anything but incredulity and ridicule," and a popular rhyme ran:

> But go not to Nahant, lest men should swear
> You are a great deal bigger than you are.

Well, the record from there on down to the very present runs just about the same. At intervals of ten years or so people along the coast of Massachusetts report the same or a similar mysterious stranger off their coasts and they come forward with some pretty convincing evidence that they at least saw something odd.

Against this is the fact that no sea-serpent has ever been caught. A ship's crew once lassoed what it thought was a serpent, but it turned out to be a long piece of seaweed.

Scientists do not say that there may not be strange monsters in the sea, but as Lockhart puts it: "So numerous have been the proved fabrications and illusions that caution is not only pardonable but necessary. The world will be convinced that the sea serpent exists when one of the tribe has been caught, brought ashore, stuffed and exhibited in a public place — and not before."

Or, as a scientist of the British Columbia Museum said a bit more sharply when Old Hiaschuckoluk was horsing around the Pacific:

"You catch him and we'll see."

EMMANUELLA
PREDICATED THIS BOOK
of which one hundred and eleven copies have been printed by S. A. Jacobs, at The Golden Eagle Press, Mount Vernon, in the month of December, 1948